Kinship

Concepts in Social Thought

Series Editor: Frank Parkin

Published Titles

Concepts in Social Thought

Kinship

C. C. Harris

University of Minnesota Press

Minneapolis

Copyright © 1990 by Christopher Harris

Published by the University of Minnesota Press
2037 University Avenue Southeast, Minneapolis MN 55414.

Printed in Great Britain

Library of Congress Cataloging-in-Publication Data

Harris, C. C. (Christopher Charles)
  Kinship/Christopher Harris.
  Includes bibliographical references and index.
  ISBN 0–8166–1893–3 (hc): $29.95 – ISBN 0–8166–1894–1 (pb): $11.95
  1. Kinship.   2. Social Stucture.   I. Title.   II. Series.
GN487.H37   1990
306.83 – dc20

The University of Minnesota
is an equal-opportunity
educator and employer.

Contents

Preface

When invited to contribute a volume on kinship to this series, my first reaction, as a family sociologist, was to suggest that this volume would more suitably be undertaken by an anthropologist. This response is symptomatic of the historical relation between the disciplines of sociology and anthropology. The study of kinship is a high-status activity central to anthropology as a discipline, where it occupies a place corresponding to the study of stratification in sociology. Sociologists do not study kinship, but 'the family'. Whereas family studies have recently acquired a new salience due to the rise of feminist thought and the interest shown by the 'new right' in family issues, they remain a relatively unprestigious activity within sociology and the effect of their current prominence has been to diminish concern with the family as a kin group and focus attention on gender relations, specifically marital relations, within the household.

The reasons for the historical division of labour between the two disciplines lies in essentially evolutionist assumptions about the nature of our society. 'Simple'/'primitive'/'early' societies were seen to be types of social formation whose structures were based on systems of kinship in contrast to 'complex', 'advanced' or 'modern' (i.e. industrial/capitalist) societies whose social life was based on the structure of economic relations. The study of kinship was central to our understanding of the first and of economic life to the second.

One of the corollaries of this view is the association of particular institutions with evolutionary stages or historical periods and the supposition that we are situated in the midst of an historical process which *eliminates* some social features and *replaces* them by others.

This corollary leads us to view 'kinship in modern societies' as an archaic survival which is doomed to extinction and has only an antiquarian interest. 'The family', on the other hand, may be seen (at least in its nuclear form) to be universal, and hence worthy of study.

I do not for a moment suggest that anyone, sociologist or social anthropologist, actually subscribes to these curious doctrines, or not at least in the vague and imprecise form in which I have stated them here. My expression of them is designed to indicate, not theories or propositions which any individual or group actually holds, but rather a meaning structure which has formed the background to the division of labour between the sister disciplines of sociology and social anthropology and influences their intellectual practice until the present, in a way which I believe is deleterious both to our understanding of kinship and of the nature of contemporary society. Because I believe this, I feel it appropriate to tackle the subject of kinship in a manner which attempts to break free from the meaning frame which has in the past inhibited not only the development of our understanding of kinship, but of the nature of human society in general. Because this book is concerned specifically with kinship – it is not a treatise on social theory – it is appropriate that I set forth, in short order, the alternative presuppositions upon which its writing is based.

A glance at the titles in the series to which this book belongs reveals that the concepts selected for discussion are of two quite different kinds. On the one hand, there are concepts that refer to culturally and historically specific ways of thinking, of which the political concepts are the best examples, i.e. socialism, liberalism, conservatism and democracy. Others refer to universal aspects of human social life (e.g. property and status), although they also connote conceptions of their referents which are culturally and historically specific.

In the case of the universals, it is relevant to ask of any given society, are there specific and distinct institutions concerned with each? If there are, it is possible to enquire further as to the autonomy of each institution relative to each of the others and to all the other institutions co-present with it. It is then possible to distinguish societies in terms of the degree of institutional specialization, and in terms of the type of institution which predominates. I do not object in principle to this way of proceeding, but it can lead to a fundamental error supposing that types of social phenomena, e.g. property, are confined to specific institutions peculiar to them. Property does not in fact refer to a class of phenomena; its referents are not discrete entities. The universality of such concepts does not depend on the universal presence of the institutions specifically concerned with them, but upon their being ineradicable *aspects* of all social relations. Because a type of institutionalized group or practice disappears or is absent from a society, it does not follow that *that aspect* of social relations is absent, nor does it excuse us from investigating its significance in the life of that society at either the theoretical or cultural level. If it were true (which it is not) that history records the replacement of feuding descent groups by antagonistic classes, it would not follow that the social relations in class societies are not still structured by kinship categories and obligations, nor that relations in descent group societies were not hierarchically organized in terms of property. The societies concerned are differentiated, not in terms of the presence or absence of structural elements, but in the manner of their articulation.

As with institutions, so with relationships. However, in the case of relationships it is only in exceptional cases that it is possible to identify them as being uniquely concerned with status, material reward or kinship, and distinctions between types of relationship can only be made by using as a criterion of distinction the meaning to which the participants accord primacy. It follows that the importance of status or material gain or kinship in the life of a given society is far greater than is suggested by a classification in those terms of the number of types of relationship which it comprises. Failure to recognize, not that some relationships are multi-stranded but that all relationships are naturally polysemic, leads to the same result as a failure to recognize the abstract character of social universals. Like the identification of universal properties with particular institutions, the exclusive categorization of relationships in terms of one meaning leads the observer to suppose that a general property belongs to a particular social sphere and to fail to understand, therefore, that property's role in the structuring of social conduct and to underestimate its importance.

Such, I hold, has been the case with kinship, and this has led scholars to suppose that its significance is restricted in modern society to the domestic sphere and that it plays little part in social life in general in advanced societies and is therefore of minor importance. The same may be said of age and gender. It is the purpose of the present work to argue that the failure to recognize the pervasive influence of kinship affects our understanding of the manner of operation of social life in that area which is regarded as the basis of modern social structure, namely economic life itself.

The evolutionary tradition furnishes us with a characterization of history in which economic institutions and relations are seen as *replacing* those of kinship in modern societies. It is but a short step from this *descriptive* scheme to a *theoretical* understanding of the difference between ancient and modern societies which presupposes that in ancient societies kinship determines social structure, while the structure of modern societies are determined by economic factors. Such a view is profoundly confused. In the first place, 'kinship' refers to a set of beliefs, values and categories which structure social action. As such, kinship is a term which refers to a social form, and specifies a set of meanings through which the social actions of individuals are to be understood. The claim that in 'primitive' societies action is structured by kinship is therefore not to claim any causal determination. The causal equivalent of this claim must refer, not to a category of meanings, but to a class of actions having material consequences. Consequently, it must refer to the determinative role of *reproductive* activities in relation to other activities. But this is not to claim that kinship institutions are dominant in primitive societies, but that family institutions are, because whatever families are, they are certainly reproductive groups. However, the whole weight of social anthropological evidence argues against the centrality of reproductive groups in 'primitive' societies, 'kinship' being sharply contrasted with 'the domestic group'.

There is therefore no conflict between the anthropological claim that social action in primitive societies is structured by kinship and, for example, the more general Marxian claim that the determinants of social structure must be sought through an understanding of the productive activities which mediate mankind's relation to nature.

It is necessary to make these rather basic and, it is hoped, obvious points because they have important and less obvious corollaries for our understanding of kinship in 'modern' societies. If the historical contrast is not between determinants but between different sets of beliefs, values and categories which give form to social relationships and activities, then to claim that contemporary social life is structured by 'the economic' is not to claim that it is 'economically' *determined*, but is to refer to the set of beliefs, values and categories through which it must be *understood*. The term 'economic' cannot therefore be specified by referring to a determinant; we cannot specify it with relation to material production, because that would have the same result as specifying kinship with reference to reproduction and the whole weight of sociological evidence is against the view that economic relations are confined to the productive sphere. As is the case with kinship, the claim that economic relations dominate the social structure of modern society is to claim that a type of meaning is central to the understanding of social actions which lie outside the sphere of activities which constitute those meanings' central reference.

Both production and reproduction are societal universals. It is this fact that gives the terms 'kinship' and 'economic' a degree of semantic stability. Equally, however, the complexes of meaning which have been socially constructed around these core meanings and extended to cover all spheres of social life in primitive and modern societies are not universal but culturally and historically specific. The debates about 'the meaning of kinship' in anthropology, which will briefly be discussed in this book, should be (but have not been) paralleled in sociology by academic debates about the meaning of 'the economic'. If it is possible to conclude with Needham that 'there is no such thing as kinship', it is equally possible to conclude that 'there is no such thing as the economic'; in contrast, that is, to 'reproduction' and 'production and exchange', respectively.

When writing the above section, I became aware that the denial of the economic 'feels' infinitely more shocking than the denial of kinship. This indicates quite clearly the sociological character of my consciousness, for sociologists are typically more concerned with comparison and generalization within one class of societies (modern/advanced/capitalist/industrial) than over the wide range of societal types which have formed the subject matter of social anthropology. The reaction of shock is due to the failure to distinguish form from content and principles of structuration from determinants of social structure. It also results, therefore, from a failure to conceive of 'the economic' as referring to a class of cultural historical individuals and from the mistaken assumption that it refers to a societal universal – the denial of whose existence would be shocking indeed. For the parallel between the core reference and cultural variation in the meanings of the terms 'kinship' and 'economic' is almost exact.

The above statement is, however, necessarily qualified by the term 'almost'. However different the specific reference of the term 'kinship' may be among those societies for which it is claimed that kinship is the dominant principle of social structuration, they do have this in common, that it is just that. However, in the case of 'economic', it is possible to argue, with Weber, that there has been historically only one set of meanings in the class 'economic' which have been capable of becoming the dominant principle of social organization, i.e. those which now structure advanced societies. Hence the contrast between kinship and the economic as principles of social organization is therefore between a class of meanings ('kinship') and one member of the class of meanings termed 'economic'. This has the important consequence that the contrast between kinship and the economic in advanced societies depends crucially, not on the general meaning of the term 'economic', but on the *specific* meaning that that term carries in such societies. Kinship relations need to be defined in relation to this particular meaning of the economic if their place in such societies is to be understood. Such a procedure does not of course allow us to address the wider question of the character of kin relations as opposed to economic relations *in general*.

I have tried briefly in the foregoing to widen the field of reference against which the discussion of kinship can proceed, by attempting to transcend not only the confused background relevances which normally frame such enquiries, but also the limitations imposed by the disciplinary aims of sociology and anthropology, respectively. It is a belief in the necessity of this endeavour that has inspired me to dare to write this work.

PART ONE

1

Kinship in Structural Anthropology

Those who, like myself, came to the study of the social sciences after completing their undergraduate studies, doubtless shared my surprise that the central concepts of the disciplines of sociology and social anthropology were rarely explicitly defined. The terms 'custom', 'practice', 'relationship', 'social category', 'social group' and, above all, 'social structure' and 'social institution' – terms without which sociological discourse would not have been possible and which defined for the initiate the distinctive character of the sociological thought of the time – had an obvious, taken for granted character, i.e. they were more like the concepts constituent of a culture, expertise in whose use one acquired by participation, than the terms of a scientific discipline subject to formal definition and whose application was governed by explicit rules and procedures.

If this was true of these contestable, second-order concepts, it was also true of the first-order concepts which defined different spheres or aspects of social life: the political, the economic, the religious. This set, sometimes referred to as the 'anthropological quadrivium', has a fourth member, i.e. 'kinship'. Of this term there is, interestingly enough, no distinctive adjectival form, and no word which can be used to connote any abstract aspectual sense: one cannot complete the set with 'kinship', in contrast to 'the familial'; 'kinship' would appear to have a purely concrete reference. The fact that a natural language term is incapable of abstract use suggests strongly that its potentialities for employment as a theoretical term are strictly limited or, worse, are positively misleading. It is not surprising, therefore, that as the theoretical and philosophical self-consciousness of the social

sciences increased after the Second World War, there was considerable debate about 'the meaning of kinship'.

This debate has been centred in British social anthropology and
there is good reason why difficulties with the concept should be of
prime concern to this discipline. As Radcliffe-Brown (1952, p. 49)
pointed out nearly 50 years ago, 'the subject of kinship has occupied
a special and important position in anthropology'. However, it is
not merely the subject matter of kinship that makes debates over its
meaning of central concern to anthropologists, but the aims of
social anthropology as a social discipline. Central to the anthropological enterprise is the *comparison* of the same phenomena in
different cultures: in Radcliffe-Brown's words, 'without systematic
comparative studies, anthropology will become only historiography
and ethnography' (quoted in Kuper, 1977, pp. 53–4). This, however, requires the solution of the problem of cross-cultural definition, an acute problem for a discipline which insists upon
understanding social action in the cultural terms of the actors and
upon explaining forms of activities in terms of their relation to other
activities co-present with them in the same culture (for a discussion,
see Kuper 1980, reprinted in Kuper, 1983).

If 'kinship' has a concrete reference, to what historical and
cultural particular does it refer? The answer must be (as with
'marriage' and 'family') that it refers to a set of practices and
relations embodying a complex of meanings specific to the societies
speaking the natural languages to which the term belongs, namely
European societies. Kinship data is obtained by the 'genealogical
method'. This consists in establishing the biological relations
between the members of the group under study and then attempting
to correlate the grid of such relations with the social relations which
structure the group. Such a procedure generates a specific type of
data and is based on the prior assumption of the universal
importance of these biological relations and of the existence of a
logical connection between the grid and its social correlates which is
assumed rather than demonstrated. The focus of many anthropological studies would be quite different if the genealogical method
was only resorted to in order to elucidate otherwise baffling features
of belief, categorization and behaviour.

There is nothing shocking in the notion that the results of
scientific enquiry are determined by the conceptual frame imposed
by the investigator on the phenomena. However, in the social

sciences, it is necessary to distinguish rigorously between concepts constitutive of the phenomena studied and the set of concepts devised by the observer for their explanation, i.e. between the 'emic' and 'etic', as they are now called (for a recent discussion, see Feleppa, 1986). It is permissible for different investigators to define 'the political' differently, as 'the political' does not necessarily refer to a type of meaning present in the minds of the subjects studied. This is not the case with kinship, which as a concept seems to straddle the 'emic'/'etic' divide. If kinship theory explicates patterns of social action, it is because the actors' behaviour is governed by concepts cognate with the observer's concept of kinship, which itself derives from European concepts of kinship. The question must arise, are not kinship studies of exotic cultures guilty of the cardinal anthropological sin of ethnocentrism?

There is therefore much at stake in the debate over 'kinship' and the term has lost its taken-for-granted, uncontested character. This part of the present work will be concerned with the history of the concept of kinship in anthropology and the debates about its meaning and significance. Before this can be even briefly attempted, something must be said about the history of anthropological thought.

The founding fathers of British social anthropology are Malinowski and Radcliffe-Brown who, together, were the originators of the 'structural functionalist' school. (Readers familiar with the sociological literature should be aware that this term has rather different resonances in social anthropology from those which it currently evokes in sociology.) The label 'structural functionalist' was devised in an attempt to specify the character of social anthropological enquiry proposed by the two men in contrast to what anthropology once was. What it once was, according to Radcliffe-Brown (1952), was an historical pseudo science depending on the method of 'conjectural history', which regarded existing small-scale societies as survivals of earlier forms of social organization ('surrogate time machines' in Gellner's phrase), and was concerned with attempting 'to explain a particular feature of one or more social systems by hypothesis as to how it [the feature] came into existence' Radcliffe-Brown, 1952, p. 49).

The structural functionalists rejected the attempt to explain cultural or social features by hypothesizing that they were caused by some past event. Radcliffe-Brown did so on two grounds. The first was that in societies without historical records, such hypotheses could not be verified. The second was that science itself was not characterized by the search for causal explanations but for structural principles of the phenomena to be studied. This has the corollary that instead of attempting to explain single items in terms of their historical antecedents, they had to be understood by locating them in the structure constituted by the pattern of relations between items which were co-present.

These assumptions were combined with the emphasis placed by Malinowski on the field study of phenomena. Once again, this follows from a distinct conception of science, viz. that science involves direct observation of the phenomena. Characteristically, the old school of nineteenth-century anthropologists had relied on reports of 'facts' from persons in the field which were then arranged in evolutionary schemes, the schemes being revised to accommodate new data. This involved a divorce between the anthropological fieldworker in the field and his master, the theoretician, in his study, to whom the facts were supplied. Malinowski insisted on the theoretical character of observation in a way that prefigures Parsons' (1949) attack on empiricism in the *Structure of Social Action*: '"facts" do not exist in sociological any more than in physical reality. . . . The principles of social organisation . . . have to be constructed by the observer . . .' (Malinowski, 1935, p. 317).

In the explanation of observations Malinowski, like Radcliffe-Brown, insisted on making connections between co-present features, rather than attempting a search for past causes, a method supplemented by an attempt to understand subjects' behaviour in their own terms. Both the approach to societies as sets of interconnected parts and an emphasis on *understanding* exotic cultures necessitated intensive fieldwork involving 'participant observation'. This revealed a disparity as well as a connection between what people do, what they say they ought to do, and what they think, or in modern terminology between actions, norms and beliefs (see Kuper, 1983, ch. 1).

This is not the place to discuss the major theoretical and methodological differences between the two men. However, despite these differences, they share what is one of the distinctive characteristics of 'classical' British social anthropology: an emphasis on action, as opposed to the study of institutions, customs myths or cultures in themselves, an emphasis to be found in the work of Radcliffe-Brown's teacher W. H. R. Rivers. This is an issue of central importance to the study of kinship and provides a convenient avenue of approach to the history of the concept.

The founding father of contemporary kinship studies is held to be Lewis H. Morgan, whose *Systems of Consanguinity and Affinity* (1870) and *Ancient Society* (1877) caused a storm of controversy. Morgan's contemporary status would have surprised Malinowski, as Morgan was regarded by Malinowski as the epitome of the evolutionary school: in Fortes' (1969) words, 'His theories, his methods, his whole approach, represented in starkest shape tendencies to which the new movement in social anthropology was most antipathetic'. Morgan's present reputation is in part the result of Fortes' rehabilitation, in which he traces the descent of Morgan's ideas through Rivers and Radcliffe-Brown to himself. Fortes' argument is that if one strips away what is still regarded as evolutionist dross, 'the . . . repugnant hypothesis of primitive promiscuity and group marriage, the preposterous scheme of stages of social evolution, the dreary addiction to kinship terminologies as an end in itself' (Fortes, 1969, p. 4), one is left with the notion of a kinship *structure* and an attempt to classify such structures in a structural (one is tempted to say structuralist) fashion. Kinship terminologies are seen as systems of categories embodying specific ideas which persist despite the change in the language in which they are expressed and the customs with which they are associated and represent selections from a limited number of alternative arrangements.

This may seem obvious to some readers; what else could kinship terms be other than the terms of a system of classification? However, as Fortes puts it, McLennan (1876) had claimed 'that classificatory systems [in Rivers' words] "formed merely a code of courtesies of ceremonial addresses" (Rivers, 1914a, p. 6)' and Kroeber had argued that 'they were "determined primarily by language" and "reflect psychology not sociology" (Kroeber, 1909, p. 84)' (Fortes, 1969, p. 9).

Morgan distinguished, in *Systems*, between 'descriptive' and 'classificatory' kinship systems. Our own system is 'descriptive' and any related person can be uniquely identified by the combination of primary terms. In contrast, in 'classificatory' systems, related persons are arranged into classes. All individuals in the same class are admitted into one and the same relationship and the same special term is applied to each and all of them. Morgan regards the descriptive system as derivative from a system of marriage between members of pairs. However, instead of arguing that different terminological systems must be understood in relation to marriage systems, he argues that descriptive systems are the result of preexisting single marriage practices, and classificatory systems of preexisting plural marriage practices – hence the conjectural hypothesis of primitive-promiscuity. However, Fortes (1969, p. 25) is insistent that 'Morgan remains, methodologically, wholly within the framework of synchronic *analysis*' [my emphasis]. It is only the 'explanations' that are conjectural and historical.

Morgan's basic data were not derived from the reports of others, but were the result of fieldwork among the American Indians. Hence, he emphasized 'the utility and necessity of kinship systems in daily life'. Kinship terminologies are not mere terminologies but used in everyday practical activities. They are not studied, nor can they be understood, as ends in themselves. This emphasis on the relation between beliefs, concepts and actions provides a link with Rivers, Radcliffe-Brown and structural functional anthropology in contrast to the concerns of cultural or structuralist anthropology.

Not only do we find in Morgan the concept of system and the necessity of understanding system in relation to action, we find also in *Ancient Society* the development of a distinction that was to become central to the anthropological study of kinship, i.e. that between 'kinship' and 'descent'. Morgan was the first to distinguish between the 'domestic' and 'political' uses of kinship. Central to this distinction is a shift of focus between *Systems* and *Ancient Society* from systems of kinship *classification* to kin *groups*.

Morgan's central interest in *Ancient Society* is the structural aspects of political organization. In kinship terms, it focuses on the 'gens' or what we should now term the 'lineage'. Morgan's extraordinary contribution here was to recognize that (in Fortes' words) 'though [the gens] was based on the recognition of kinship relations, it was a civil rather than a domestic unit' and this led Morgan to distinguish between 'kindred' and 'gens'. Morgan was the first to point out that 'the family' cannot be the basic unit of societal organization, because families must comprise persons of both sexes, and if ties through both sexes are recognized, then kinship cannot provide for the establishment of exclusive groups. For kinship to provide the basis of societal organization, lineage groups, based on the principles of unilateral descent, are required. Such groups and systems of relationships do not and cannot have their origin in the domestic sphere where relations are 'naturally' bilateral. Both classificatory systems of classification and unilineal systems of group formation are therefore seen as cultural distortions of a natural state of affairs. Such 'distortions' are to be understood in terms of the wider societal uses to which kinship relationships are put. Therefore, Morgan warns us against an identification to which sociologists are prone and from which even anthropologists have not been exempt, i.e. the identification of kinship in its widest sense with domestic group membership and interpersonal relations. The category of kin having obligations to a given Ego (kindred) must be radically distinguished from groups wider than the domestic group, having a political or economic character, which are none the less defined in kinship terms. It is precisely these considerations which have given rise to the contemporary debate over the meaning of kinship. For just as kinship straddles the *emic* and *etic* categories, so it permeates other social spheres and institutions.

We have in Morgan a prefiguring also of what are currently considered to be the three main divisions of kinship studies: classification, kinship groups and institutions, and marriage or 'alliance'. Enough has already been said, however, to suggest that the understanding of kinship is not advanced by considering these areas separately, as it is precisely the interrelation between these aspects that constitutes the phenomenon termed 'kinship' and defines the debate about its nature.

Morgan's work suffered an eclipse during the last decades of the nineteenth century and only regained prominence when taken up again by W. H. R. Rivers. Rivers remained faithful to 'conjectural history' as the title of his best known ethnographic work – *History of Melanesian Society* (1914b) – indicates. But 'in his fieldwork Rivers had discovered and revealed to others the importance of the investigation of behaviour of relatives to one another as a means of understanding a system of kinship' (Radcliffe-Brown, 1941, 1952, p. 51). In 1909, an American anthropologist, A. L. Kroeber, published an article in the *Journal of the Royal Anthropological Institute* which brought him into conflict with Rivers. Like Radcliffe-Brown, Kroeber objected to evolutionary anthropology seeking explanations in unverifiable past events, and using single traits as both *explanandum* and *explanans*. However, the crux of the debate concerned systems of kinship terminology. Rivers held that kinship terminology is, so to speak, the precipitate of social *action*: that particular features of terminology result from particular features of past social organization. Against this, Kroeber held that terminologies were primarily linguistic, i.e. cultural phenomena – 'terms of relationships are determined primarily by linguistic factors and are only occasionally, and then indirectly, affected by social circumstances'. The connection for Kroeber was between the structure of collective thought and its linguistic expression, but he denied any connection between terminology and institutionalized action, let alone the determination of terminology by behaviour postulated by Rivers.

Today our sympathies must be with what Kroeber asserted and with his denial of Rivers' behavioural determinism. Yet in the long run, Rivers' position was to prove more influential than Kroeber's. Radcliffe-Brown disagreed with both the protagonists in the ensuing debate (for Rivers' position, see Rivers, 1914b) on the grounds that both parties regarded causal explanation as the touchstone of science. What Radcliffe-Brown argued against, however, was not merely the search for causal *historical* explanations, but also the relevance of the issue of causality in both Kroeber's *and* Rivers' positions. Radcliffe-Brown learned from Rivers (following Morgan) that there was an intimate *connection* between terminology and behaviour but denied that the connection was causal. He accepted Kroeber's claim of a connection between thought and terminology, accepted that it was not causal, but denied that this precluded any attempt at explanation. Radcliffe-Brown's approach can best be conveyed by an extended quotation from his 'The study of kinship systems' (1941, 1952, pp. 61–2):

> For Kroeber the kinship nomenclature of a people represents their general manner of thought as applied to kinship. But the institutions of a people also represent their general manner of thought as applied to kinship and marriage. Are we to suppose that . . . the way of thinking about kinship as it appears on the one hand in the terminology and on the other hand in social customs are not merely different but are not connected? This seems to be in effect what Kroeber is proposing . . .
> My own conception is that the nomenclature of kinship is an intrinsic part of a kinship system just as it is also, of course, an

intrinsic part of a language. The relations between the nomenclature and the rest of the system are relations within an ordered whole . . .

Kinship systems are made and remade by man, in the same sense that languages are made and remade. . . . A language has to work, i.e. it has to provide a more or less adequate instrument for communication, and in order that it may work it has to conform to certain general necessary conditions. . . . A kinship system also has to work if it is to exist or persist. It has to provide an orderly and workable system of social relations defined by social usage. A comparison of different systems shows us how workable kinship systems have been created by utilising certain structural principles, and certain mechanisms.

It is quite clear that Radcliffe-Brown, far from rejecting Kroeber's linguistic orientation, is extending and criticizing it. Our knowledge of linguistic and kinship systems is constituted by our grasp of their structural principles, but these principles must also be seen to be adequate, to work (function?) in providing an instrument for communication and an orderly and workable system of social relations, respectively. Kinship terminology can no more be divorced from kinship institutions than can language from speech acts. However, the connection between the orderly system of social relations, kinship terminology and a general manner of thought is not an external, causal one, but internal and logical in character.

What does Radcliffe-Brown mean when he says that a kinship system has to 'work'? The answer to this question is of quite extraordinary importance. It is to provide a distribution of rights and duties between the members of a population. These rights and duties are attached to different categories. The categories, which the kinship terminology names, must be logically prior to the rights and duties attached to them, or otherwise there would be no need for the categories in the first place. The system of classification ensures that the distribution is orderly and constitutes a system, but it also has to provide for the effective discharge of the duties which it distributes. Or, to put it another way, it provides a form which must be adequate or be appropriate to or 'fit' its content. But if this is so, kinship would appear to be a purely formal principle of social organization without a specific content of its own.

This conclusion was far from Radcliffe-Brown's intention. To the modern reader, there is a certain paradox in Radcliffe-Brown's approach. In the classic essay from which we have already quoted at

length, Radcliffe-Brown attempts to explicate the notion of kinship. Knowing that Radcliffe-Brown's work is largely concerned
with the complexities of unilineal systems and classificatory terminology which extend beyond the domestic domain, and that he
emphasized the importance of jural relations as correlates, if not
determinants, of kinship terminology, we are surprised to discover
that Radcliffe-Brown's attempt at definition begins with a description of the elementary family. However, on closer inspection, this
term refers not to a domestic *group* but to a *category* of kin whose
members stand in direct relation to each other (primary kin), those
relations (parent–child; sib–sib; husband–wife) constituting the
elements of any system of kinship and affinity. Any given ego
belongs typically to two such 'families'; that into which he was born
and that created by his marriage. 'This interlocking of elementary
families creates a network . . . of genealogical relations, spreading
out indefinitely' (Radcliffe-Brown, 1941, 1952, p. 52).

What we have here is a description of *categories* rather than
domestic *groups*; though categories such that, whether bounded or
not, their members' relations to one another are characterized by
intimacy or familiarity. Each ego is seen to be at the centre of a
ramified network of relations which can be specified in terms of the
elementary genealogical or biological relations. Radcliffe-Brown
continues: 'It is relations [culturally] recognised in this way that
constitute what I call a kinship system' (loc. cit.).

It is necessary at this point to juxtapose Radcliffe-Brown's
conception of kinship with Malinowski's. Malinowski's contribution to the study of kinship has been the less influential of the two
and is generally regarded as centring on two related elements: the
'principle of legitimacy' and 'the extension theory of kinship'. The
principle of legitimacy states that in all societies a social father:

> is regarded by law, custom and morals as an indispensable element of
> the procreative group. The woman has to be married before she is
> allowed legitimately to conceive, or else a subsequent marriage or an
> act of adoption [is necessary to give] the child full tribal or civil status.
>
> (Malinowski, 1930, p. 24)

This principle is important, less for what it asserts than for the
implicit distinction which it sets up between *pater* and *genitor*. For
members of a society to recognize a man as a child's genitor is not
the same as according that child membership of the appropriate

social group. For this purpose, the child must have a jural or ritual father or 'pater'. The ascription of social fatherhood is not only not based on genetic fatherhood; it is not even based on the existence of a relationship between persons who play the role of father and child to one another – the relationship follows from the ascription, not the ascription from the relationship. Malinowski therefore recognizes the logical priority of categories to rights and duties.

This principle, therefore, runs entirely contrary to Malinowski's espousal of an extension theory of kinship. Malinowski (1930) wrote that 'the family is always the domestic institution *par excellence*. . . . The clan, on the other hand, is never a domestic institution. Bonds of clanship develop much later in life . . . out of the primary kinship of the family'. Hence the relationships precede the categories and descent arises out of an extension of the sentiments generated within the domestic domain to the societal level, not in some remote historical period, but in each generation. But Malinowski held, as did Radcliffe-Brown and Fortes after him, that 'family relations' or those of 'filiation' or of 'kinship' (as opposed to descent) were universally bilateral. Descent is reckoned unilineally. How can unilineal relations be an extension of bilateral ones? Malinowski's answer was to identify bilateral kinship (as did Morgan) with nature and see the use of the unilineal principle in descent group formation as the result of the distortion of nature by culture. However, this leaves culture as a mysterious and unexplicated cause and fails to explain the wider use of elementary kin relationships, which is the whole purpose of extension theories of kinship in the first place.

This muddle confuses the rational and the empirical and is not one into which Radcliffe-Brown fell. As we have seen, Radcliffe-Brown saw the relationships characteristic of the domestic sphere providing the elementary logical elements of wider structures, rather than the domestic sphere generating a dynamic of sentiments which serves as a cause of those wider structures. For him, the wider was logically rooted in the narrower, but was in no sense caused by it. The connection is therefore a structural connection between elements in the same cultures. Any explanation of intersocietal differences between wider structures cannot be *culturally* explained, because the structures between which the differences exist do not form part of a wider cultural whole; rather, they have to be sought in terms of the different uses to which these wider structures are put, which provide the criteria for deciding whether or not they *work*. For Radcliffe-Brown, the central problematic of kinship in descent group societies concerned the balancing of affectual bilateral ties to close kin which are generated through domestic group membership with the duties and obligations of descent group membership and allocated on unilineal principles.

In view of their differences, it is at first sight surprising that Fortes should have commented that, in both Radcliffe-Brown's and Malinowski's approaches, 'the actual relations of persons in the parental family was the starting point' (Fortes, 1969, p. 48). Fortes' point is, of course, a structural one: for both men, 'the kinship system is envisaged as a bilateral network of recognised dyadic relations radiating outwards from the elementary family' leading to a dyadic analysis 'which accords well with a genealogical interpretation of kinship relations' (Fortes, 1969, p. 49). However, kin categories and descent groups are not agglomerates of dyadic relations; their members do not relate to each other in terms of chains of relationships, indicated by sequences of elementary terms, upon which their membership is based. Rather those relationships are those of identity and sameness. Fortes (1953, p. 30) noted that in societies with a low division of labour and little social individuation, 'there is nothing which could so precisely and incontrovertibly fix one's place in society as one's parentage', i.e. one's location in the network of genealogical relations. However, if the function of kin location is to provide individual identity, the function of descent group organization – whether of lineage or clan – is to *abolish* social differences between members of a subgroup, to use kinship despite itself to overcome individual differences. This is possible because, for day-to-day practical purposes, recognition of membership of descent groups is not dependent on genealogical knowledge, though that knowledge may have resulted in the original attribution. In Fortes' (1969, p. 50) words: 'people are located in status positions relative to other status positions by the system of terminology and custom not [by location . . .] in specifiable genealogical positions'. A failure to recognize this fact Fortes terms 'the genealogical fallacy', which, he claims, leads the observer to fail to recognize that a given ego has not one but two statuses derived from 'kinship': an individuating one derived from bilateral kinship and a 'class' status derived from descent group membership.

We may think of descent groups as the classes of simple societies. I use the term 'class' here advisedly. I do not of course use it in the basal Marxian sense with reference to a system of productive relations, nor in the other usage which defines it, *inter alia*, as an *open stratum*. I use it rather in the superstructural Marxian sense to refer to relationships in which participants orient to each other solely as category members or, to use old-fashioned terminology, as 'bearers' of structural locations. Class relations in sociology are counterposed to kinship, age, gender and communal relations on the grounds of the universalistic characteristics of the first, and of the particularistic character of the remainder. It is salutary to be reminded, therefore, that descent relationships are universalistic relationships based on kinship. Descent categories are also corporate groups, as Radcliffe-Brown (1935, 1952) eventually came to recognize, and the institutions which define them are 'not customary patterns of interaction between persons [as suggested by the genealogical model] but . . . the vehicles of interests and requirements that flow from the overall constitution of society' (Fortes, 1969, pp. 50–1). In this sense also, descent groups are like classes: they comprise individuals occupying the same position in societal structure whereby they share common interests which may conflict with those of other categories of the same type and which are expressed through organization.

Kinship cannot therefore be simplistically opposed to the economic and political (or religious) aspects of social structure; nor can it be identified with the domestic, as opposed to the public, nor even with the particularistic as opposed to universalistic relations, since kinship would appear to straddle the dichotomies in which sociologists think, rather than constituting one side of them.

Today, it would be accepted that Fortes was correct in his judgement that the major advance in kinship theory after Radcliffe-Brown 'has been the analytical separation of the politico-jural domain from the familial, or domestic, domain within the total social universe of what have been clumsily called kinship based systems' (Fortes, 1969, p. 72). To this movement of *analytical* separation Fortes was, of course, himself the principal contributor. Fortes is often credited with distinguishing 'kinship' and 'descent': the former bilateral and arising out of the domestic and reproductive sphere; the latter being concerned with the allocation of individuals to corporate groups whose significance is jural and political (for Fortes' own view, see Fortes, 1969, ch. 10). This does an injustice to the sophistication of Fortes' position and at the same time is positively dangerous if applied to our thinking about kinship in first world societies. For example, in a recent work on research methodology on kinship, Barnard and Good (1984, p. 34) claim that in urban settings 'kinship tends to be much less evident in the public domain: kinship relationships become above all *domestic* relationships' [emphasis in the original]. Among the many things which are wrong with this statement is (1) the supposition that the public and domestic spheres exhaust the universe of significance of kinship and (2) the tacit identification of the public sphere with the politico-jural, economic sphere.

Fortes' use of 'domain' is unfortunate, because it predisposes to the reification of the domestic and political, etc., when his intention is to make an analytic distinction. In his rightly celebrated article on unilineal descent groups, Fortes (1953, p. 29) argued that we should 'think of social structure in terms of levels of organization'. He goes on:

> We can investigate the total social structure . . . at the level of local organisation, at that of kinship, at the level of corporate group structure and government, and [at] that of ritual institutions. . . . One of the problems of analysis and exposition is to perceive and state the fact that all levels of structure are simultaneously involved in every social relationship and activity.
>
> (*idem*)

The distinction between kinship and descent is not between separate spheres or separate sets of relationships but between two aspects of a relationship. In a patrilineal descent system, a man's relation to his father has two elements: it is both a relation between close kin and a relation between two members of the same politico-jural group. Conversely, the relationship between the same man and his mother also has two elements: close kinship and different politico-jural group membership. Fortes' point is not, as Dumont (1971, p. 76) has claimed, that unilineal descent is an aspect of the political jural order *and not* of kinship. Rather, Fortes' point is that descent group organization has to be understood 'from the point of view of the total social system and not from that of an hypothetical ego . . . consanguinity and affinity are not sufficient in themselves to bring about these structural arrangements . . .

descent is fundamentally a jural concept' (Fortes, 1953, p. 30). However, Fortes goes on to connect the domestic and political through an examination of lineage segmentation:

> it is through the family that the lineage (and therefore society) is replenished by successive generations; and it is on the basis of the ties and cleavages between husband and wife, . . . between siblings, and between generations that growth and segmentation take place in the lineage. Study of this process has added much to our understanding of well-known aspects of family and kinship structure.
>
> (Fortes, 1953, p. 33)

Descent groups are not *either* jural *or* kin groups. Nor are 'families'. Relations in both groups have politico-jural and kin aspects: this must be so because all individuals are simultaneously members of both types of group and descent groups are formed on the basis of principles that can only be expressed in the same language that is used to specify relationships arising out of procreative activities. The same concepts are used both to individuate and unite and, as a result, dyadic relationships are capable of evoking simultaneously both the identity and the difference of the parties to them. Similarly, all individuals, in addition to being members of exclusive corporate groups to whom they owe political loyalty, are also linked by ties of filiation to kinsmen in other groups, thus binding together the major groups into which the society is divided and providing a principle of the segmentation of such groups. Fortes drew attention to the importance of bilateral relationships in maintaining the structure of descent group societies by coining the term 'complementary filiation' to refer to the recognition of ties through the parent through whom descent is not traced.

A furious debate then raged between Fortes and Edmund Leach about how the ties connecting different descent groups should be conceptualized. Such ties are created by marriage between the descent groups so that the kin of one spouse become the affines of the other. Hence, in descent group societies having rules of exogamy (marrying out of one's own group), which prescribe or specify the preferred group from which spouses are to be drawn, different descent groups may be thought of as being each other's affines (relations through marriage). This is the position of those such as Leach who have been termed *alliance* theorists. *Descent* theorists see the significance of such relations resulting from marriage as creating, in the next generation, *kinship* ties between the groups. Non-anthropologists find this dispute difficult to understand, but it can be explicated by reference to common experience of familial relations in our own society. How should a man perceive his wife's parents: as his parents *in law* (his wife's kin) or as his children's grandparents (his kin's kin)? Clearly, they are both, as are the relations between exogamous intermarrying descent groups, and if this is what the debate is about it is nothing in Fortes' words but 'pure casuistry'. Therefore, some other consideration must be involved to explain the dispute between alliance and descent theorists in anthropology.

The issue here is the general sociological one concerning the nature of societal solidarity. Descent group societies are, in Durkeimian terminology, segmentary societies exhibiting solidarity through likeness, relations between the segments as well as within them being cemented (according to Fortes) by kinship. The members of any stable population whose members intermarry become over time linked by a web of kin ties, and the categories 'inhabitant' and 'kin' become identical. This web of kinship is cross-cut by economic and politico-jural divisions superimposed upon it. The stability of the structure is guaranteed by a balance between unifying and dividing principles, between kinship and descent.

The alliance school, in contrast, sees the unifying principles to lie not in kinship but in exchange. In classical sociological thought, as in our own culture, 'exchange' carries the sense which it has in economic theory. It is a dyadic relationship which depends on the equivalence of what is exchanged. If exchange *is* equivalent, then it becomes unintelligible unless the parties to it are differentiated and the two flows involved in exchange are qualitatively different. Hence exchange has not been traditionally seen as a mechanism of solidarity in segmentary (i.e. undifferentiated) societies, but as *the* integrative mechanism in *differentiated* ones. The alliance school drives a coach and horses through this convenient dichotomy by proposing that exchange is the integrative mechanism in *segmentary* societies.

This view derives from the work of the French structuralist anthropologist Claude Lévi-Strauss, who claimed in his seminal work *Elementary Structures of Kinship* (1969) that the ultimate origin of social solidarity lay in the incest taboo. The vexed question of the universality of the taboo need not detain us here. We need only note that in no society do people mate with their primary kin, and in many societies the prohibition is much more extensive. Given this fact, however it is to be explained, in all societies people have to seek mates outside their *natal* group. Hence, if anything is a society, it is composed of a plurality of exclusive groups which exchange mates. The most primitive form of social solidarity is therefore that of exchange.

This view may appear extremely shocking to the non-anthropological reader. It is less so to anthropologists. What is fundamental to exchange, most anthropologists would agree, is not the principle of *equivalence* but the principle of *reciprocity*, i.e. the principle that the acceptance of a gift creates an obligation to respond with a gift. Just as the 'economic' as we understand it in our own society and culture is but one specific cultural form of a social universal, so is 'equivalence-exchange' (analysed by classical economic theory and its successors) only one culturally specific form of exchange. It *is* exchange because it is based like all forms of exchange on reciprocity. What is being claimed by the alliance theorists is that exchange in the general (not culturally specific) sense, is the most primitive form of solidarity.

As far as the dispute with descent theory is concerned, the 'exchange' (alliance) interpretation preserves the distinctness of the *boundary* between descent groups, while the descent theory blurs it. Lévi-Strauss' (1969) analysis makes it possible to 'disentangle a small number of simple principles from the . . . diversity of rules of marriage', whereas descent theory does not, and his means for so doing is the distinction between generalized and restricted *exchange*. However, it must be noted that logically, the simplification by means of reference to the concept of exchange depends on a specification of the diversity of rules of marriage in kinship terms; e.g. the most effective form of general exchange is one resulting from a marriage rule prescribing that a man marry his mother's brother's daughter, a member of a specified kinship category. In other words, when one marries into a different lineage in this way, one is marrying into one's kindred, though out of one's descent group, a circumstance which markedly differentiates marriages in descent group societies from marriages in non-descent group societies like our own.

One of the difficulties of this debate is a lack of agreement as to what it is about. Fortes (1969) specifically rejects the view that it is about whether kinship or marriage is the more important determinant of systems of kinship and affinity. Fortes' objection is that by focusing on marriage rules, Lévi-Strauss conceives of descent groups as natal groups – as a sort of extended primary kin group (an 'extended family'?) – and thereby ignores their politico-jural character. Alliance theory does not 'reckon with the politico-jural determinants of kinship, descent and marriage relations', (Fortes, 1969, p. 83), and in so doing ignores the significance of such relationships to the participants.

> The theoretical paradigm set up by the observer and the pragmatic paradigm used by the actors in a social system are not antinomic as Lévi-Strauss and others seem to maintain . . . a good theoretical model . . . must correspond to the pragmatic model.
>
> (Fortes, 1969, p. 82, n. 36)

While the whole question of marriage rules and relations between descent groups has little relevance to kinship in first world societies with which this book is chiefly concerned, the debate can be seen as reflecting the divergent tendencies in the conception of kinship which this chapter has already chronicled. First, there is the tension between the 'emic' and 'etic' conceptions of kinship; between the genealogical grid of biological relations on the one hand, and the meaningful social relationships built upon them and the conception of kinship that informs them in the culture concerned on the other. Secondly, there is the problem of relating conceptions and relationships whose ultimate reference is to procreative activities and the domestic domain, to conceptions in relationships which belong to other domains. It is, essentially, these two problems which lie at the root of the questioning of the meaningfulness of the concept of kinship itself, and it this debate which forms the subject of the next chapter.

However, there is a third issue which is perhaps more important than either, as it divides cultural and structuralist anthropology from social anthropology. And that is the issue of the relation between a structural principle or classification system and the practical uses to which it is put.

2

The Concept of Kinship

This book is concerned with 'kinship' and not with 'family'. Families are generally regarded as domestic groups within which reproduction takes place. Reproduction is obviously a human universal being a natural characteristic of a species. There is therefore a universal question that may be asked of every society: what are the social rules which govern the activities and relationships which are concerned with reproduction? In this case, there is no difficulty in specifying the meaning which is central to any feature of social life which we claim to be familial or reproductive. Both member and observer categories must carry reference to this universal activity if those categories are to be properly termed familial/reproductive. The rules, roles, relationships and groups which carry that reference in any given society are to be regarded as cultural and social variations on a universal natural theme. Reproductive relationships are simultaneously both cultural and natural. They cannot be specified without reference to activities intrinsic to reproduction, but do not necessarily involve any system of classification of persons.

However, this book is not concerned with reproductive/familial institutions, but with *kinship*. In primitive society, moieties, clans and lineages are not reproductive groups. In our own society, the cooperation of 'kin' is not restricted to the reproductive and domestic sphere and does not necessarily involve the tasks characteristic of that sphere. In both types of society, significant relationships depend on a system of *classification*, and this system of classification determines which and in what way the relationships generated by the reproductive process are significant for social action. It is therefore customary to distinguish between biological

or physical relatedness and social kinship, using the first to provide
an *etic* grid for charting the *emic* relationships of the second.
However, because all possible physical relations are not recognized
for the purpose of social action, one cannot simply say that 'kinship'
refers to the cultural categories for the description of biological
relatedness. As Needham (1960, p. 96) states: 'the distinction
between biology and the notion of descent is the *pons asinorum* of
descent systems'. Hence anthropology undergraduates are frequently taught that 'Biology is one matter and descent is quite
another, of a different order' (Needham, 1960, p. 97). However, for
Gellner (1960, 1973, p 170), this constitutes one of many 'misleading slogans about the alleged independence of physical and social
kinship'. It is designed to express the 'crude point – that physical
and social kinship are not identical', while ignoring 'the slightly
subtler point concerning their essential connection' (Gellner, 1973,
p. 171).

For Gellner, the term 'kinship' refers neither to a set of roles,
statuses and relationships (i.e. the social aspect of kinship) nor to
the physical kin position (i.e. location in a network of biological
relationships). 'It is the connection between [the two] that constitutes much of the study of "kinship structure"' (Gellner, 1973,
p. 171). To put this another way, it is the *connection* between the *etic*
categories of biological relatedness and the *emic* categories of
kinship terminology that constitutes 'kinship' for Gellner, so that
both observer and participants each have a role in constituting a
given set of relationships as kin relationships, but these two roles
are logically independent. It is the conclusion by the observer that
the structure of a set of related terms systematically overlaps the
grid of biological relatedness that warrants the claim that that set is a
set of *kin* terms.

Gellner sets out his position in response to an attack by Needham
(1960) on an article by Gellner (1957) in the *Philosophy of Science*,
entitled 'Ideal language and kinship structure'. The original article
by Gellner was not about the nature of kinship or the meaning of the
term, but about developing a language which could specify,
formally, the properties of the grid of biological relatedness which
the structure of kinship terms systematically overlaps. In so doing,
Gellner had to distinguish and relate biological and social relatedness: '"kinship structure" means two separate things though
anthropologists are right in not normally separating them' (Gellner,

1957, p. 235). The debate, sparked by the article, has continued as if the 'two separate things' were any given set of kin terms with their attached behavioural prescriptions and the paradigm of biological relatedness generated by the permutation of elementary genealogical terms. That is to say, it has proceeded as if what Gellner was distinguishing was the social and the natural/biological/physical. This was not, in fact, the case.

The first of Gellner's 'two separate things' was 'which kinds of matings actually occur'. The point here is that the biological relations subsisting between members of a given population – the web or network of biological relatedness – are not the product of random mating, but are structured, since all types of mating are not allowed, equally preferred, or have the same probability of occurring. The plurality of 'physical' relationships that exist within a population is therefore a social product, a structured *set*, not a mere aggregate. Hence the first of Gellner's 'separate things' is not a natural (as opposed to social) but a socially structured set of natural relations.

The second of Gellner's referents of the term kinship structure is the *correlation* of social roles with statuses in the kinship structure in the first sense of the term. The point is that *each* side of Gellner's dichotomy is a *relation*: in the first place between form and content – the socially determined 'shape' of biological relations; in the second case it is a relation between location in kinship structure in the first sense and the set of rights and obligations and relationships constitutive of social structure. At the phenomenal level it is not of course possible to distinguish these 'things'. It is only possible to specify the rules of mating which determine the kinds of matings which actually occur in terms of members' set of names for kinship positions, which carry with them a specification of the rights and duties subsisting between the positions which they define. The separation is only possible by virtue of the recourse by the observer to a set of *etic* categories for specifying mating patterns.

The essence of the debate does not therefore concern the relation between the natural and the social. It is rather a debate about whether or not the natural can provide the basis for the construction of a privileged (not an ideal) descriptive language for the purposes of cross-cultural comparison. Such a language may be termed 'privileged' if it is not the culturally determined product of the observer's own society. If it were not privileged in this way, the observer would be guilty of imposing the categories of his or her own culture upon those of others, and thus fall into the sin of ethnocentricity. I wish to claim that this issue is central to the debate because Gellner's original distinction between 'two separate things' depends on a fundamental presupposition. This presupposition is that it is in principle possible to describe kinship structure in the first sense in a language which is logically independent of that language constituted by the *emic* categories used by members. Only if that presupposition holds, is it possible to claim that kinship structure in Gellner's second sense is the correlation of social roles with kinship structure in his first sense. In both his original article and in his reply to Needham, Gellner is quite clear that this relation/correlation is, as the term correlation suggests, a synthetic, contingent relation. It must be, since if it were a necessary one, all societies would have the same kinship system.

The gulf between Gellner and Needham is nowhere more clearly manifest than in Needham's claim that what Gellner calls 'sociological predicates' 'cannot be simply contingent: the categories of classification and the jural status of person defined and ordered by it are inseparable parts of one and the same system' (Needham, 1960, p. 100). If we are talking about an *emic* system, this is clearly correct. Gellner is not; he is talking about the relation between an *etic* system and the *emic* one.

Gellner is therefore entirely correct to allege that Needham has totally misunderstood his original article. He is also right to suppose that any attempt to abolish the relation between the natural and the social in the definition of kinship leads to absurdity:

> . . . anthropologists frequently say that, for instance, kinship is of great importance in simpler societies, or that in some societies of this kind a man's position in the social structure is determined by his birth. Suppose for a moment that Needham were right, and this meant (merely) social kinship and (merely) social birth, and that the connection of these with physical kinship or birth were merely contingent or sociologically irrelevant. The meaning of the statement cited would then degenerate into saying something almost wholly vacuous, namely that simple societies have some kind of structure of relationships, and that a man's social position is determined by something.
>
> (Gellner, 1973, p. 165)

Could not Gellner's opponent reply, however, that what is being claimed is that social positions in simpler societies are conceived by their members in terms borrowed from physical kinship? No, says Gellner, since the only way of knowing that some terms in a language *are* kin terms 'is that their application does overlap with physical kinship' (loc. cit.).

It becomes evident that, whether or not it is possible to construct a privileged *language* for the specification of kinship structure, it is necessary in order to save the term kinship from vacuity that the term itself has a privileged status, i.e. that there must be some test of whether a set of terms has a 'kin' reference independently of members' conception of the characterization of that set, and Gellner's test is the systematic overlap with physical kinship. However, there is no natural reality out there, which can be apprehended independently of our concepts of it, called physical kinship, and the notion of this objective test depends on the unquestioned acceptance of *our* conception of physical relatedness. All universals in anthropology have had to contend with this difficulty and debates have raged over the definition of religion and marriage. However, in the case of kinship, we can be led into supposing that concepts which have a natural reference avoid the logical difficulties attached to the establishment of other transcultural definitions. Unfortunately, they do not.

The way out of this basic difficulty is to claim that a term has meaning both through its relation to other (*emic*) terms in the same system and through its reference. The referent of the term may be classified in *etic* categories without doing violence to the authenticity of members' *emic* concepts. This, however, has major consequences for the understanding of the meaning of kinship. It leads us to assume that the universal function of kinship is *cognitive* and not normative. If we claim that two systems of relationships in two different societies are both kinship relationships, we are claiming that they are systems which classify and differentiate on the basis of reference to physical kinship. We are not claiming that the relationships which flow from the relationships thus defined are political, jural or religious; nor that they are personal, affective, domestic or private; nor public, rational, categorical or instrumental. To claim that the relationships concerned are kin relationships is to claim merely that they derive from a system of categories and positions which have reference to 'physical kinship' however conceived. The only thing kinship systems necessarily have in common is that they are cognitive systems employed for the ordering of social relationships which have reference to some aspect of 'physical kinship'.

Gellner's approach involves not only two relations; it also involves not one but two overlaps and this can only be seen clearly when we recognize the essentially cognitive nature of kinship systems. The grid of relationships which flows from the nomenclature of a kinship system must on the one hand systematically overlap the grid of biological relations, and on the other it must systematically overlap the grid of social relationships of the society concerned. To claim the centrality of kinship in simple societies is to claim that this second overlap is extensive if not exhaustive. If it were exhaustive, then all a person's rights, duties and obligations, category and group memberships and the relations which flow from them, could be inferred from knowledge of that person's location within the kinship system. In complex societies, this is not of course the case. Indeed, very little can be inferred from the knowledge of kin position, and what can be inferred tends to refer to the domestic sphere. As a result, our cultural-historical understanding of kinship in the West in the twentieth century tends to ascribe to kinship relations a particular content which is, loosely, familial.

This ascription blinds us to the pervasive influence of kinship in social domains other than the domestic. However, to assert the pervasiveness of that influence is not to dissent from Gellner's position or from the claim that the second overlap (between the kinship system and the totality of social relations) is not extensive. Gellner is concerned with the *systematic* overlap of three *structures*, i.e. three ordered sets of relations. It is the ordering of the sets and the systematicity of their overlap that makes possible the inference from location in the biological grid to location in the kinship grid, and from location in the kinship grid to location in the structure of social relations.

Gellner's insistence on the contingency of the relation between these three sets of relations should not be misunderstood. He is not claiming that the relation between any actual two relations is contingent, but that the overlaps of the sets of relations is contingent. It is a contingent matter whether a society traces descent in the male or female line; it is a contingent matter whether relationships thus traced are used for the ordering of economic or political or religious relationships or all three. Once one knows the principles governing the overlap of kinship categories with biological ones, and social categories with kinship categories, the existence of actual relationships can be predicted, as they are entailed by those two sets of principles taken together. What those principles are is a contingent matter of fact, but given those principles the existence of relationships follow necessarily.

In our own society, there is no principle governing the overlap of kin relations and the other institutional domains. However, this does not entail that there is no overlap, but only that it is not systematic, and hence no inference can readily be made from knowledge of kin location to location in the social structure. The matter may be put this way. Anthropologists ask not merely about the principles governing the overlap of the set of kinship categories with the biological grid; they also enquire as to the social uses to which the *society* puts the kinship system. Both types of question are equally pertinent in respect of complex societies studied by sociologists, but the second question cannot enquire in such cases as to the uses to which the *society* puts the kinship system, but must investigate instead the social uses to which its *members* put it.

It is now necessary to return to the vexed question of the 'privileged' status of the concept of kinship. Here it is necessary to distinguish rigorously between the concept of kinship and the concept of its referent which is central to Gellner's definition. Gellner's specification of the meaning of *the anthropological concept of kinship* is not only not part of British culture; the controversy which it stirred up indicates that it is not part of the culture of social anthropologists either. It is therefore an intellectual construct which has to be understood in terms of the aims of its author and the conditions under which it is designed to be used.

The conception of the *referent* of the *etic* term kinship and the *emic* reference of any set of terms to which it is applied is, however, quite a different matter. Gellner's definition would not be intelligible unless it referred at some point to phenomena intelligible through concepts shared by his readers by virtue of their participation in a common culture. Barnes' contribution to the debate makes this clear. Who, he asks, is the genetic (as opposed to social) father of the child? He answers that 'It is he who supplies the spermatozoon that impregnates the ovum that eventually becomes the child'. (Barnes, 1961, p. 297). In other words, Gellner appears to be claiming that the referent of a set of kin terms is the network of

biological relations as understood by Western science. The universal reality to which the concept of kinship is held to refer is in fact
that reality as understood by a specific culture. This does not, I
submit, invalidate the claim that the concept of kinship has a
privileged status, since this claim is based on the universality of that
reality rather than of any particular way of conceptualizing it. The
structure of that reality is that the birth of a child requires the sexual
conjunction of a male and a female. Provided that the cultural
understanding of human reproduction in all cultures (including our
own) is predicated upon that structure, we are dealing with a
culturally recognized universal. The presupposition that all reproduction requires such a conjunction is of the same order as Marx's
presupposition as to the pragmatic priority of the satisfaction of
bodily needs to all other human activities. It is no more necessary to
go into detail about spermatozoon and ova to secure that universal
reference, than it is necessary to specify the content of kinship
relations to recognize them as kinship relations.

The difficulty raised by the absence of a culture-free conception
of biological relatedness is methodological rather than epistemological. We recognize kinship, according to Gellner, by establishing
the systematic overlap of kin relations with the grid of biological
relations. In practice, this is done by establishing the actual web of
biological relations and the kin terms applied to them. However, we
cannot establish what that web is. What the anthropologist does,
and it is all that can be done, is to correlate kin relationships with
socially recognized biological relations. Barnes points out that we
should not confuse the anthropological distinction between the
social (jural) *pater* and the socially recognized *genitor* with the
distinction between kinship (social) and biology (natural). In
practice, it is the systematic overlap between putative kin relationships and the web of genealogical (i.e. socially recognized biological) relations that warrants the application of the term kinship, i.e.
it is the relation between *pater* and *genitor* rather than *pater* and
genetic father; it is 'between social and physical kinship as culturally
perceived' (Barnes, 1961, p. 298).

The word 'culturally' suggests that a new problem arises, namely
the stability of the reference of the term kinship. For if physical
kinship is perceived differently in different cultures, then the nature
of the overlap between the biological grid and the system of kinship
cannot be compared between cultures, because the culturally

invariant stable point of reference has disappeared. However, this does not raise epistemological difficulties. It does not matter how the facts of life are culturally conceived by members provided those conceptions have the same structure as our observer conception of biological kinship. The difficulty we have just encountered is, rather, methodological, and derives not from differences in cultural conceptions but from differences between methods employed by members of different societies to ascertain biological relatedness. However genuine this difficulty may be, it does not really matter for general anthropological purposes that the web of genealogical relations is not identical with that of biological relationships, though it would matter, for example, if one was conducting a study of the effect of different kinship systems on the transmission of genetic defects. Indeed, Barnes makes the point that Needham rather than Gellner is correct if one takes the claim of the former that kinship is social and not biological to be a claim that the study of kinship is concerned not with the study of human reproduction but with popular and legal conceptions of reproduction and the uses to which they are put.

Therefore, we may summarize the position as follows. To specify the nature of kinship in a manner which permits the term to be applied crossculturally, it is necessary to distinguish (a) the total set of social relations constituting social structure, (b) the set of relations constituted by kin terms, (c) the set of genealogical relations and (d) the set of biological relations.

Any set of members' terms is a set of kin terms if it overlaps both (a) and (c) systematically, and any set of members' terms is a set of genealogical terms if it overlaps both (b) and (d) systematically (cf. Gellner's reply to Barnes; Gellner, 1963, *passim*). It is a criterion of systematicity that it is possible to infer from a location in one set the location in another set in those cases where overlap is claimed to obtain. In the case of kinship terms, every member of the set must overlap with the set of genealogical relations and with the set of social relations. However, it is not required that every social relation must correspond to a kin relation, otherwise all relationships in all societies would be kin relations. Nor is it necessary that every genealogical relation overlap with every kin relation, otherwise every society would have the same kinship system.

The anthropological concept of kinship is not part of the culture of any given society and its necessary reference is not to a cultural conception of biological relatedness but to the reality itself. The fact that this reality cannot be recognized except through culturally specific concepts of biological relatedness, does not destroy the universality of the concept of biological relatedness provided that all culturally specific concepts of biological relatedness have the same basic structure.

Why has this last consideration been added? Because for a set of terms to be kinship terms, those terms must themselves refer to physical kinship. In other words, it is not enough for the anthropological concept of kinship to have reference to physical kinship; the set of terms which are thereby termed 'kin' terms must *connote* as well as denote physical kinship. It is not clear to the present author whether Gellner would agree on the necessity of such connotation, since his whole argument concerns the necessity of the denotation. What is clear is that the opposition between Gellner and his opponents concerns the relative importance of the ideal and material aspects of social life.

Gellner's position is materialist. Institutions are related to each other 'through the medium of the physical' (Gellner, 1963, p. 249) as well as being related through the ideas or values which they embody:

> The mistaken doctrine that only social matters are of concern to social anthropology provides a prop for a quite unnecessary kind of social and conceptual relativism to the effect that every society can only be understood through its own concepts, etc. . . . [anthropology] sees every society as coping with and functioning within a natural environment.
>
> (Gellner, 1963, p. 250)

> [It] is concerned with the social impact of physical facts as they are and not merely as they appear.
>
> (Gellner, 1963, p. 251)

Gellner's position is also that of a comparative anthropologist. His opponents take the position of ethnographers working within a particular society. Hence Beattie replies to Gellner by complaining that many *emic* kinship terms are not connotative of physical kinship. Moreover, complains Beattie, ethnographers do not in practice use the denotative 'overlap' criterion to establish that a term is a kin term, since at the stage of their enquiry they cannot have got to know anything about physical kinship and hence cannot establish any overlap. What the ethnographer does, according to Beattie, is to 'isolate the field of institutionalised social relationships in which the people whom he is studying use the *language* of kinship' (Beattie, 1964, p. 101; original emphasis). To this Gellner would presumably reply: 'But how do you know that a term is a part of the language of kinship if it is not descriptive, at either the connotative or denotative level, of a biological relation?'

There is only one possible answer to this question and that is because of the distinctive content of the relationship to which a putative kin term is applied. However, Beattie rightly rejects this solution in a celebrated passage which is worth quoting *in extenso*:

> To . . . say that a social relationship is a kinship one is to tell us nothing at all of its content. The whole point about kinship relations for the social anthropologist is that they *must* be something else, for example political, jural, economic or ritual. Kinship is the idiom in which certain kinds of political, jural, economic, etc. relations are talked and thought about in certain societies. . . . [Roles] are subsumed under 'kinship', not at all because of their content, which has to be defined in social terms, but because of the idiom in which they are thought of and talked about in the society being studied.
>
> (Beattie, 1964, p. 102)

I can find nothing in Gellner's work which would lead me to suppose that he disagrees with the view put forward here. Beattie is listing a set of types of what Gellner called in his 1957 article 'social predicates'. Beattie is focusing on the overlap between the set of kin terms and the social relationships constituting the structure of the society. But that only sharpens the point of the question, attributed to Gellner above. How does one recognize the idiom of kinship if the relationships to which it is applied are political, ritual, etc., in content and the alleged kinship terms have no reference to biological kinship? Beattie gives us a clue, but in so doing betrays the difficulties of his position:

> The Bantu term *nyinarumi* usually translated 'mother's brother', does not mean this; literally it means 'male mother' or 'mother man'. . . . Kinship terms are not the names of genealogical connections even though they may be associated with such connections. They are names of categories, sometimes groups, of people, socially defined.
>
> (Beattie, 1964, p. 101)

Now neither Gellner, nor anyone else, has ever claimed that if a term is to be a kinship term it must be the *name* of a genealogical connection. If Beattie is claiming that kin terms are used to name people and not biological relations, he is certainly correct. 'Neighbour' is not the name of a spatial relation but is used to denote a member of a social category between whom certain obligations exist. However, the term neighbour logically refers to the fact of physical proximity, and that fact is a criterion of the application of the term. Gellner's argument concerning kinship is of this kind. Remove the logical reference to biological kinship/physical proximity, and the terms 'kin'/'neighbour' are emptied of their semantic content and become merely the names of any social relationship of the parties thereto. Why does Beattie bother to tell us that *nyinarumi* is translated 'mother's brother', and why *is* it so translated? It is so translated because it is the term applied by members to persons who are accounted as mother's brothers according to the rules for the attribution of genealogical relationships in that society. The systematic overlap between the term and a genealogical position is the warrant for our calling it a kin term.

Let us consider the converse of this case. Christians refer to God as their *father* and the church as their *mother* and to each other as *brothers* and *sisters*. Since the italicized terms both connote and denote biological relationships, we may regard them as kin terms, and assert that Christian linguistic practice utilizes 'the idiom of kinship' to describe ritual relationships. Are those relationships kin relationships? If Beattie asserts that they are, then he is consistent. However, it is universally agreed that they are not kin relationships but ritual ones, and no amount of utilization of the idiom of kinship makes them so, because there is no necessary biological relationship between the persons whose relationships have been described by the idiom.

If a term is to be classified as a kin term, it must refer to a type of biological relationship, and if a type of relationship is to be held to be a kin relationship, it must be built upon a type of biological relationship. If this logical condition is waived, kinship simply disappears. At this point in the argument, Schneider attempted to rescue Beattie from the embrace of Gellner to which his assertion that kinship relations lack any specific content had driven him (Schneider, 1965). Schneider believes that Beattie is mistaken in supposing that kin relationships are empty of kin-specific content and suggests why Beattie makes this mistake:

> He may only have looked for it [the kin-specific content] in those so-called 'primitive societies' in which it is hardly possible to see the kinship for the economics and politics which obscure it. Perhaps if he had looked for it in England or America or France he might have found a society where kinship is laid bare to analytical inspection by virtue of the fact that it has been refracted from the economic and political and ritual and religious functions with which it is so closely associated elsewhere.
>
> (Schneider, 1965, p. 181)

Unfortunately, he gave us no clue as to the nature of this specific content. The reason for this is that Schneider is moving from social to cultural anthropology, a distinction which Schneider was later to put in the following way:

> . . . the symbols and meanings of the beliefs and premises about human reproduction, of bio-genetic relationship and so on [function to cope] . . . with the problems of meaning and with the maintenance of solidarity and of particular patterns of solidarity. They provide a meaningful social order and social life in this sense . . . this . . . is the distinctly *cultural* question. . . . The question of how man copes with the facts of human reproduction is a distinctly sociological or social system or *social organisational* question of a very different kind.
>
> (Schneider, 1972, p. 47)

From the mid-1960s onwards, the discussion of the question of the nature of kinship splits into two separate streams: those of cultural and social anthropology. On the social anthropology side the debate recounted above produced a degree of anxiety about the study of kinship in the discipline and the discipline of anthropology itself. The annual general meeting of the Association of Social Anthropologists agreed with Leach that they needed to get back to 'firm anthropological ground' and decided that this meant 'kinship' and resolved to devote a conference to that topic. The result was a conference volume commencing with three critical articles, in the first of which Needham concluded his discussion of kinship with the iconoclastic *ex cathedra* pronouncement that 'there is no such thing as kinship, and it follows that there can be no such thing as kinship theory' (Needham, 1971a, p. 5). Basically, his argument is that kinship refers to a particular way of allocating rights and transmitting them from one generation to the next. *Anything* can be transmitted in this way, and anything that is so transmitted need not be. 'These jural systems and their component statuses can be genealogically defined . . . but the method of description does not entail any particular property in what is described' (Needham, 1971a, p. 4). The argument here is close to that of Beattie. Kinship relationships have no kin-specific content. Of course, they logically refer to genealogical relations but that reference has no social significance, because it does not follow that 'the relations in question are genealogical or that they are so conceived by the actors'.

Needham's article and that of Southwold (1971) make clear the reason for the prior debate and the centrality of kinship to anthropology and the uncertainity about it. This hinges on the relationship between 'kinship' and 'descent'. Let us suppose that we distinguish between 'kinship' (the bilateral network of social relations generated by the reproductive process) and 'descent' (the use of genealogical principles to form exclusive categories and groups for the allocation and transmission of social position). If we so distinguish these two orders of phenomena we must also connect them, because we have to say that descent involves the use of kinship for societal purposes. So descent is both the opposite of kinship and a use of it. We can escape this difficulty if we distinguish between, on the one hand, the relations of reproduction and their extension and, on the other, the use of genealogical principles to order the societal allocation and transmission of rights. Much of the debate has been clouded by the failure to make this distinction, since of course there is no content necessarily common to relations generated by reproduction and those created for jural or political purposes, even though both sets of relations systematically overlap the genealogical grid.

Southwold (in Needham, 1971b) goes beyond this distinction, however, by distinguishing 'parentation' and 'congeniacy'. He defines 'congeniacy' as the defining property of 'those social relationships in which appropriate behaviour is characteristically perceived as similar to that expected in familial relationships' and 'kinship' in essence as congeniate relations which are mapped on to relations of 'parentation'. It follows that the establishment of a genealogical relationship does not warrant the presupposition that it is congeniate, nor the classification of a relationship as congeniate the presupposition that it is mapped on to a genealogical (parentate) relationship. The first disjunction is relevant to descent. Because membership of corporate political, economic or religious groups is allocated genealogically, it does not follow that relationships between members have any kin-specific content, i.e. they are not necessarily congeniate. Conversely, because relationships are congeniate, it does not follow that they are allocated on the basis of parentage. Hence neither intra-descent group relationships nor neighbouring relationships are kin relationships; kin relationships are congeniate relationships allocated on the basis of parentage.

When Southwold specifies the characteristics of kin relationships he adopts without acknowledgement two of Parsons' pattern variables, i.e. kin relationships are ascribed and diffuse – he could (and should) have added 'affective' and 'particularistic'. He should, moreover, have properly made these characteristics those of *congeniency*. The overlap between parentage and congeniacy is contingent, but probable, since statuses ascribed by birth must hold between parentates. In smaller settlements, relationships will be given, not chosen; persons interacting in one domain will interact with the same person in others. Relations based on propinquity will, therefore, tend to be diffuse. However, if the settlement is isolated its inhabitants will also intermarry and hence be linked by parentate relations. Hence the inhabitants will be bound by a web of relationships which are both parentate and congeniate. However, it does not follow that those relations are kin relations unless the congeniate relationships are allocated on the basis of parentate relations rather than merely empirically overlapping them.

This requirement shifts the determination as to whether or not a set of relations are kinship relations from the observer to the *society* concerned. What is characteristically absent from Southwold's discussion is any recognition of the activity of society members as a determinant of how these relationships are conceived. The whole point of allocating rights is that these rights can be cashed, in practice, in appropriate circumstances. Actualizing a right which flows from a status involves getting the person who has the corresponding duty to acknowledge his occupancy of the status. Where persons are related by the occupancy of a plurality of statuses, they have the choice of which interpretation to put upon the relationship. And here, at the level of praxis, rather than structure, the language of 'idiom' is highly relevant. Demands that another discharge a duty may be couched in a number of different idioms of which reference to parentage is one, and that reference constitutes the idiom as that of kinship.

Southwold makes two crucial moves in his discussion of kinship. The first is to say the essence of kinship is simply the system of kin terms; or as I have put it in the discussion of Gellner above, that it is merely a cognitive device. Kinship must refer to a set of cognitive ordering categories, certainly. But for Southwold it also refers simultaneously to a type of normative prescription associated therewith. Southwold is only able to make this stipulation by adopting the classic distinction between kinship and descent made by Fortes and to which some attention was given in Chapter 1 (see pp. 21–2). The sociological predicates of genealogy when used as a principle of descent group formation are necessarily diverse and vary between societies of whose populations they are a principle of structuration. Kinship, however, structures the social fields of its members, not the population of a society: its primary significance is personal rather than social. It is of universal social significance because of the universality of the reproductive process to which it refers.

It is not surprising, therefore, that the notion that kinship, not descent, *does* have a distinctive normative content, is taken up again in the *Festschrift* for Fortes edited by Goody (1973), since it was Fortes who first emphasized the distinction between kinship and descent to insist on, as Bloch (1973) notes, the moral character of kinship, a morality which cannot be reduced to self-interest. In his contribution, Pitt-Rivers (1973) notes that late in his career Fortes articulated a concept which underlies most of his work. In sharp contrast to Needham's 'there is no such thing as kinship', Fortes writes:

> the domain of familial and kinship relations, institutions and values, is structurally discrete . . . founded on principles and processes that are irreducible . . . a critical feature of this domain, intrinsic to its constitution and distinctive of its manifestations in social life is a set of normative premises . . . focussed on a general and fundamental axiom which I call . . . amity.
>
> (Fortes, 1969, pp. 250-1)

The chosen relations of friendship and the prescribed relations of kinship are subclasses of amicable relationships which, in Pitt-Rivers' words, imply a moral obligation to feel – or at least feign –

sentiments which commit the individual to actions of altruism, to generosity. The moral obligation is to forego self-interest in favour of another, to sacrifice oneself for the sake of someone else. However, Pitt-Rivers fails to stress sufficiently the particularity of relations of amity. He properly writes 'in favour of another' not 'in favour of others'. We are not therefore talking of Christian *agape* but of something of which *agape* is a shocking violation, precisely because it universalizes altruistic obligation hitherto restricted to particularistic relationships. The downside of amicable relationships is hostile relations with all those with whom one does not have amicable relations. The ideological warrant for kin as opposed to friendship relations is, according to Pitt-Rivers, the notion of consubstantiality, of metaphysical identity: 'like breeds like', he writes, 'in every system of thought'. For Pitt-Rivers, kinship is therefore a relation of amicability which is warranted by a biological idiom of identity of substance, however expressed. It is no accident, therefore, that the Christian ideal of universal amicability can only be expressed through a familial idiom: the brotherhood of man and the fatherhood of God.

This attempt to distinguish kinship as a subcategory of genealogical relations and invest it with a type of normative content has to be distinguished from Schneider's enterprise in cultural anthropology. Schneider distinguishes three levels of social analysis: observable patterns of behaviour, the normative system and the cultural system. The second is abstracted from the first and 'consists in the rules and regulations which an actor should follow if his behaviour is to be accepted by his community or his society as proper'. The cultural system:

> consists in the symbols and meanings embedded in the normative system. . . . By symbols and meanings I mean the basic premises which a culture points for life: what its unity consists in; how those units are defined and differentiated; how they form an integrated order or classification; how the world is structured; in what part it consists and on what premises it is conceived to exist, the categories and classifications of the various domains of the world of man and how they relate one with another, and the world that man sees himself living in.
>
> (Schneider, 1972, p. 38)

Studying the American kinship system as a cultural phenomenon, Schneider (1968) claims that 'the defining features . . . are first, shared biogenetic substance and, second, a code for conduct which I have characterised as diffuse, enduring solidarity'. This seems to put him squarely among Fortes and his followers – Southwold, Bloch and Pitt-Rivers. The defining features of Schneider's approach is that he then sees these two features as the expression in the domain of kinship of two much wider and more general American cultural categories, i.e. the order of nature and the order of law. The significance of the biological reference does not derive from its literal reference to the facts of life; its meaning is given rather by its position in a set of cultural categories, the other members of which stand in contrast to it. Its cultural function is to symbolize social relations of diffuse and enduring solidarity.

In essence, Schneider's argument is an old one, i.e. that 'kinship' is a product of the anthropologists' practice of mapping social relationships on to the genealogical grid, instead of investigating the meanings inherent in relationships in terms of the 'units' of the culture of the society concerned. Kinship, he claims, does not exist, because in the way that Morgan and his followers have used it, 'it does not correspond to any cultural category known to man' (Schneider, 1968, p. 50). The proper way to proceed is not to start with the genealogical grid and interpret kin terms, behaviour, norms and meanings as if they must have reference to it, but rather to start with the symbol system and ask how the different aspects of the fact of biological relatedness as we understand it are signified in the system of the culture concerned. The relation of such symbols to the culturally specific symbolization of other universals – what *we* call economics, politics and ritual – must then be investigated. Only when that has been done are we equipped to distinguish between the different domains of social life distinguished by the cultural system of the society. Whether there is any domain that corresponds to kinship as defined by Morgan and his followers thus becomes a contingent matter, and the content of relations within such a domain a cultural particular not a universal.

A study of Schneider's work, especially his *Critique of the Study of Kinship* (1984), makes it clear that behind Schneider's position lies the basic presupposition of the *Geisteswissenschaften* or cultural sciences that knowledge in this field involves establishing the relation between the scientist's culture/epoch and that of the other society/culture/epoch studied. This is not strictly one of comparison by use of an observer model applied to both. Rather, it involves taking the categories of the observer culture as a reference point. Cultural work, therefore, requires first the analysis of the symbolic structure of one's own culture; hence Schneider's return from foreign fields and his study of American culture (Schneider, 1968). Schneider is at pains to minimize the radicality of his critique by emphasizing at certain points the distinction between social and cultural anthropology, and it is quite correct to suppose that these two subdisciplines have different problematics and much of the difference between Schneider and those whom he terms 'Morgan and his followers' derive from his choice of a different problematic. However, Schneider's disclaimers are to a degree disingenuous, since though his adoption of a cultural position may leave the enterprise of *social* anthropology intact, his critique has profound implications for social anthropological method. He is claiming not merely that social anthropologists' aims are different, but on the one hand that their *methods* of the study of kinship are fundamentally misconceived – a critique of traditional *ethnography* – and on the other that the attempt to establish general categories for *analysis* in anthropology (as opposed to categories which establish problematics which guide enquiry) is misconceived.

For Schneider, kinship is not the name of a phenomenon but of a set of questions. Arguments detailed in this chapter all assume that kinship phenomena exist universally and the question is – what do they have in common? We have seen that there are two types of answer. One refers to the systematic empirical overlap of genetic relations, genealogical relations, kin terms and social relations. The other insists on the meaning of relationships and requires either that they have a kin-specific content or a reference to genealogical relations or both. Schneider belongs to neither camp, since he rejects the *assumption* of the proposition that all societies define a domain which can be termed kinship, and that in all societies parentage is highly significant in terms of the cultural value assigned to it and the social uses to which it is put, and does not regard the truth of the proposition as warranted by the results of the genealogical method.

The weakness of his approach is his use of the Parsonian distinction between the cultural and social systems to establish two different enterprises called social and cultural anthropology. This prevents him from examining the way in which society members use cultural symbols to define different social domains and classify relations within them. He therefore retains one of the weaknesses of traditional anthropology, its failure to cope with the dialectical relationship between structure and action. This is central to understanding the place of kinship in our own society where the empirical overlap between relationships comprised by the different institutional domains recognized by the culture provide members with choices about how those relationships and even the domains themselves are to be defined.

PART TWO

PART TWO

3

The Character of Kinship

Part 1 has attempted in extremely narrow compass to locate the concept of kinship within the intellectual discourses in which it has figured and to demonstrate its currently contested character. In so doing, it has been necessary to distinguish between 'kinship' and 'descent', i.e. it has been necessary to distinguish between relationships arising out of the procreative process and relationships between members of corporate groups which employ classifications of genealogical relationship as principles of recruitment. The former structure the social field of the individual; the latter constitute a principle of structuration of the society. Before employing this distinction, it is necessary to note that it should not be used to imply an opposition between relationships having a specific content and relationships which have a structuring, ordering function. While the content of descent relationships is variable, kin relationships have both a distinctive content and a structuring function. The difference between kinship and descent concerns what is ordered: individuals' social fields in the case of kinship, and the distribution of other types of rights and statuses in the case of descent.

In the rest of this book we shall be concerned with kinship rather than descent. This does not imply that we shall not be concerned with the relation between kin relations and relations in other social domains; rather, we shall be concerned with the overlap between kinship and other social domains, where (to follow Gellner) the overlap is not systematic and when (to follow Schneider) there is no sense in which the relationships in those other domains are *culturally* defined with reference to either procreation or genealogy. The concentration on kinship at the expense of descent means that we are better able to investigate the character of kinship, because to employ the term in its *restricted* sense frees us from trying to find a content necessarily common to relationships which belong to different social domains or arise out of the performance of different social functions.

The last sentence of the previous paragraph concludes with two alternative phrases, the first vague, the second precise. They represent two alternative ways of classifying the social relationships which constitute, at the phenomenal level, what both sociologists and social anthropologists term 'social structure'. The second, precise criterion of classification concerns the function of the relationship, i.e. its effect in maintaining the social group of whose social life it is part. This study has already noted that classically societies have been considered to possess four aspects, which go under the name of the anthropological quadrivium which comprises, in 'emic' terms, 'the political', 'the religious', 'the economic' and 'kinship'. In 'etic', functionalist terms the quadrivium connotes four functions. The first two are concerned with the maintenance of a distribution of authority and power and the maintenance of a symbolic order. The last two are concerned with the material and biological reproduction of the members of the social group. These four functions provide the basis for the classification of four types of social relationships, so that it becomes possible to distinguish, for example, councillor–voter relationships as political, relationships between church members as religious, employer–employee relationships as economic and relations between siblings as kin relationships.

The reader will be swift to note the banality of these illustrations. What else could a relationship between church members be but a religious relationship? This banality derives from the fact that the quadrivium is merely the elevation, to the academic level, of a classificatory scheme employed by members of Western European societies for the understanding of their own social life. The validity of the concepts which constitute it derives from their being cognate with the concepts internal to the very institutions and relationships to which they are applied. It follows that while it may be valid to suppose that, if any social group is to persist, the four functions specified must be fulfilled; and while questions as to how they are fulfilled are questions of universal application, it does not follow that the .members of all cultures distinguish relationships with reference to which of the four functions they are associated. The quadrivium is therefore of limited use for the classification of relationships, whatever other uses it may have.

So far we have spoken merely of 'the classification of relationships'. It is necessary to distinguish, however, between the classification of actual relationships and types of relationships or institutions. It does not follow from the fact that members of a given society distinguish between *institutions* in terms of the quadrivium, that they necessarily so classify actual relationships, or indeed that they classify relationships at all. This is a difficulty with which survey interviewers are not unfamiliar. If one asks a respondent to list their social contacts within a given time period and then requests them to specify their social relationships to each, the respondent frequently experiences difficulty. This is so not merely because the relationship may be multi-stranded, the contact being simultaneously a neighbour, friend, relation, employer and co-religionist (for example), but also because the universality of the functionalist questions derives not from the universal existence of social entities (groups/institutions/relationships) which specialize in the performance of those functions, but from the terms 'power', 'resources' and 'meaning' connoting universal *aspects* of social life; aspects which are the universal attributes not merely of 'societies' but also of the institutions and relationships which constitute elements of their structure. Families, churches and work establishments have their own polities; families, work establishments and political parties have their own systems of ritual and belief; and families, churches and political parties have their own economies. The significance of an actual relationship, and hence its category membership, is therefore not fixed but variable. Even in cultures where the quadrivium operates as a scheme for the classification of institutions, it does not follow that it can be used to classify actual (as opposed to typical) relationships.

However, it cannot be claimed that *kinship* refers to either a theoretically necessary feature of all societies or to a universal aspect of all social relationships and institutions. What is logically universal is reproduction. The existence of social recognition of biological relations, i.e. the existence of genealogical relations and their use as a mechanism for the allocation of rights and duties, is a purely contingent matter, as is what rights and duties are so allocated. While it is possible (however mistaken) to define institutions and relationships in terms of their functions, kinship relationships cannot be so defined, because they are not the means of the performance of any of the four functions. It is possible to define the family in functional terms as a reproductive group and hence the relationship between group members as reproductive relations. To speak of kin relationships is, however, to refer to a class of relationships which include the reproductive group but extend beyond it into other social domains.

The term domain allows us to escape the straightjacket of functionalist definitions and through it we can refer to whatever distinctions between different areas of social life are made in a given culture. However, a cultural approach does not help us to solve the problem of specifying the character of kinship, and this is so not because domain classifications differ between cultures but because it is characteristic of kinship relations that they are not confined to a single domain. *Kinship is not a domain word*, whether domains are distinguished 'etically' by the observer as among functionalists or 'emically' by members of the culture concerned.

We are therefore faced with two problems: the classification of social relationships in general and of kinship relationships in particular. The first problem concerns not merely the analysis of any given society, but the specification of the character of different societal types. We cannot accept that the historically distinctive characteristic of our own society is that it is structured by economic relationships and not by kinship unless we can establish the cross-cultural applicability of not only the category 'kinship' but also of the category 'economic'. And yet the truth of this observation seems both self-evident and important. However, there is a way out of this difficulty and this involves accepting *two fundamental methodological principles*. The *first* is that we can only understand other societies through concepts which derive from our own culture and the recognition of this fact is not to accept the inevitability of ethnocentrism but to take the first and most important step towards its avoidance. Once we recognize that the quadrivium is a Western European classification, we become free to use it as a list of questions to ask of all societies without supposing that the members of those societies themselves employ that classification. The *second* is that any classification lumps together, not merely logical individuals which differ in their particularity, but also *subclasses* of phenomena. Hence, we may follow Gellner in

employing the notion of systematic overlap between the genealogical grid, kinship nomenclature and social roles and statuses in
distinguishing kinship from non-kinship relationship types. This
'etic' definition is necessary to make cross-cultural comparison.
Within that broad category, however, subcategories may be
distinguished with reference to the cultural meaning attached to
kinship relationships, and this will involve members' classifications
of social domains rather than the imposition of our classification.

However, these two principles do not apply merely to kinship.
They apply equally to economic phenomena. Any 'etic' classification of the economic will subsume culturally distinct types of
economic action and relationship. Recognition of this fact then
leads us to an explanatory principle which is that it is by the
investigation of the differences in the cultural content of economic
and kinship phenomena (etically defined) that the structural weight
accorded to economic relations in modern societies can be explained. To claim that the basic structure of modern societies is
economic is not to claim that it is constituted by economic
relationships of the same type as those found in pre-modern
societies. Equally, the claim that kinship structures the social fields
of individuals but is not the key principle of societal structure in
modern societies is not to claim that kin relationships in modern
societies are of the same type as those in societies where they do
constitute the key structural principle. It is precisely because in each
type of society both kin relationships and economic relationships
belong to different species of their genera that their structural
function is different.

We shall at this point follow tradition and custom and accept not
only that modern societies are not structured by kinship but also
that kinship relations are characteristically pre-modern. It then
follows that we need to characterize kinship relations in such a way
that they have a character which contrasts with characteristically
modern social relations. Before doing so, however, it is necessary to
return to the 'domain' point. In the above discussion, it has been
assumed that cultures vary in the way they divide up social life into
different domains. Here it is necessary to make a more fundamental
point, namely that cultures vary in the extent to which different
domains are separated in practice. One of the characteristics of
modernity is conventionally held to be the separation of the
different domains – of the state from civil society, of the family from

the economy, of religion from the family and the state. Relationships within the *distinct domains* of the polity and the economy are held to be distinctively modern relationships; relations within the reproductive and religious domains are held to be pre-modern.

The contrast between the two pairs of domains, representing pre-modern and modern types of social relationships, was elegantly formulated by Talcott Parsons using what he termed the 'pattern variables' (Parsons, 1951, pp. 76-109). These are a set of distinctions concerning the values embodied in different types of action and relationship. They are as follows: universalism *vs* particularism, affective neutrality *vs* affectivity, achievement *vs* ascription, specific *vs* diffuse significance. In universalitic relationships, the actor orients towards another primarily in terms of the other's category membership; in particularistic relationships, the actor gives primacy to the particular relation in which he stands to the other. This distinction neatly grasps one of the elements of the contrast between kinship and descent: though particularistic relations are used to allocate persons to descent groups, members orient to each other primarily in terms of category membership; the actual genealogical relation is ignored. In the case of kinship, however, the relationship depends on the exact genealogical relationship involved. In modern societies, class relationships are universalistic.

In affectively neutral relationships, the other person has no emotional significance to the actor – or if there is such significance, the emotion must not be expressed. Professional–client relationships are of this kind. In relations of amity (kinship and friendship), affect and its expression is central to the relationship.

In relations characterized by an achievement orientation, the actor orients to the other in terms of the other's performance. Relations between the buyers and sellers of labour power are of this kind. In contrast, when the orientation is ascriptive, primacy is given to the qualities of the other which are ascribed. Relations between the genders and between races are ascriptive. In any relationship the significance of the other party may be specific; the relationship between a customer and a checkout girl is of this kind. Not only does the significance of the relationship not extend to domains other than that within which the interaction occurs, it does not even extend beyond any given piece of interaction in its own domain. Alternatively, a relationship's significance may be so diffuse that there can be no occasion nor any domain in which the relationship is not significant. Relationships between identity groups, e.g. social classes (in T. H. Marshall's, 1934, sense), or ethnic groups, are of this kind.

Now economic relationships in modern society may be defined as universalistic, affectively neutral, achievement-oriented and specific. In contrast, kin relationships are particularistic, affective, ascribed and have a diffuse significance. All members of the category 'sons' do not stand in the same relationship to all members of the category 'mothers': the relationship only exists between pairs as a result of the particular genealogical relation subsisting between pair members. Mothers and sons are expected to have and show affection for each other. The relationship does not depend, like a contractual relation, on the performance of the parties to it; rather, the performance depends on the relation. There is no social context or social domain in which the existence of a mother–son relationship between two parties is not relevant to their action.

Kinship and economic relations constitute polar opposites. The relation between these opposites is, however, an interesting one. Each constitutes a coherent and opposed set of social values; each constitutes a culture in itself. Yet they inhere in the same society at the same time. Their co-existence would, according to Parsons, be impossible but for the central structural feature of modern society: the separation of the different aspects of social life into distinct domains. Parsons uses the 'necessity' of such separation to assert the functionality of the system of nuclear family formation and the dysfunctionality of the formation of domestic groups including members other than the spouse and immature children. The functionality of the nuclear family system consists in the fact that only one member (the husband) participates in the economic domain, so that family members never interact in the economic sphere and hence are never required to obey, simultaneously, contradictory role prescriptions. However, this would seem to imply not merely that the system of family formation is nuclear – that the family has shrunk in modern society to its nuclear core – but also that the *kinship* system has become identical with the elementary family. However, Parsons does not assume this, but rather ignores the problem posed by extrafamilial kin. He does so because he makes the unwarranted empirical assumption that nuclear families are highly geographically mobile across large distances and that, consequently, the chances of encountering extrafamilial kin in the economic sphere are small.

If we accept Parsons' characterization of economic and kinship relationships and his argument that the two sets of relationships constitute antagonistic cultures co-present in the same society, but deny his assumption that they do not empirically come into conflict, then we must conclude that the economic domain is continually under threat of invasion by a set of values inimical to it, and not only values inherent in kin relationships. For cultural values rival to those of the economic domain are not only found in kinship relations. Relationships based on ascriptive characteristics – age, gender, ethnic group, territorial group, confessional allegiance – cannot be segregated from the economic sphere. In the 1960s and early 1970s, it was easy to mock Parsons' concern with avoiding this conflict of values. However, events in Eastern Europe are now demonstrating that the threat to the operation of a modern economy posed by the penetration of cultural values alien to it is very real.

The threat ascriptive relationships pose to other types of relationship derives from their diffuse significance. To claim that kinship relationships have a diffuse significance is to draw attention to one aspect of the character of *kinship* which has already been remarked upon. It is not a domain. It has no specific content. It is a set of structuring principles which can be used by the society or the individual for any purpose. Economic relationships, precisely because their significance is specific, do not similarly invade the 'kinship domain', since there is no such domain, because kinship relationships have no substantive content by reference to which such a domain could be defined.

At this point, it must be noted that it is not 'the economic', *in general*, that is subverted by kinship, but rather that subcategory of economic relations which is characterized by rational capitalist economic criteria in the Weberian sense, whose distinguishing features are the orientation of action to a single end, namely profit maximization based on a rational system of calculation; Parsons' pattern variable scheme is an attempt to specify the values upon which such action depends. For the ideal typical capitalist, or commissar for that matter, when acting in that capacity, the significance of people is purely economic: they are merely the bearers of their economic functions (specificity). What matters is not *who* they are, but how they perform those functions (achievement). Conversely, it behoves the capitalist to behave in such a way as to optimize performance unswayed by sentimental considerations (affective neutrality) and to behave to all the members of an economic category in the same way irrespective of their particular relationship to him (universalism).

This ideal typical model of economic behaviour can be put otherwise in more emotive terms, and has been. What is germane to the argument of this chapter, however, and necessarily not articulated by Parsons, is the primacy given to category membership as against total social identity. This is not adequately expressed by the universalism–particularism distinction, which so elegantly expresses one central difference between class and kinship relations. The distinction which is not adequately expressed in the Parsonian scheme could be described as that between one-dimensional category membership and multi-dimensional personal identity. Kinship relations are *personal* relations, i.e. relations between total persons. The point here is not that there is no context in which the fact that your role partner was your mother was not relevant (diffuse significance). The point is that there is no context in which a person's relationship with their mother is unaffected by their mother's other, non-kinship attributes. Personal social relationships – even when, as in the case of kinship (as opposed to friendship), the relationship flows from the occupancy of a status – are those relationships in which the parties orient towards the person rather than the status occupied or the activity performed. We have now reached a point at which it begins to become possible to say something more about the character of kinship relations than merely that they are genealogically based and structure individuals' social fields.

The opposite of universalistic becomes *personal* rather than particularistic. All relationships which are 'personal' necessarily have a diffuse significance, since if the person, not the status, carries significance, then that significance cannot be confined to a specific social domain. If a relationship is personal, affect is likely to involved, and whether or not the norms governing it endorse the expression of affect, they are unlikely to inhibit it. We may define, therefore, one type of relationship as simultaneously personal, affective and diffuse. Two other qualities of relationship may also be distinguished within the personal category, the ascriptive and particularistic. The first poses a problem. If the orientation is towards the total person as opposed to one social dimension, then that person's significance may depend on their being chosen as a party to the relationship rather than upon their possession of an attribute, whether ascribed or achieved. The dichotomy, therefore, needs to become a trichotomy: ascribed, achieved, chosen. With regard to the second quality, the opposite of particularism ceases to be universalism, and particularism is seen as a particular method of ascription.

Kinship relations appear to be unique in that they are personal, diffuse, affective, ascribed and particularistic. They are distinctive, in that unlike friendship relations they are ascribed and not chosen. Unlike relationships between members of territorial groups which are also diffuse, ascribed and particularistic, they are personal and affective. Unlike gender, race and age relations which are ascribed and diffuse, they are personal, affective and particularistic.

While the above system of classification is somewhat tentative and suffers from certain ambiguities imported with the Parsonian pattern variables, it does suggest that it is possible to distinguish kin relationships from other relationships, not only of a totally different kind like economic relationships, but also from other similar types of relationships, and to do this at the purely *formal* level without specifying any specific *content*. However, the categories used derive from an attempt to specify the distinctive character of rational capitalist economic relations characteristic of modern society, and therefore involve a specification of the character of kinship from a specific standpoint in culture and history.

It is now necessary to consider the question of whether it is possible to specify any common content to kin relationships. We have already seen in Chapter 2 that Southwold (1971) views kin relationships as a subcategory of *congeniate* relations and that Pitt-Rivers (following Fortes, 1969) regards them as a subcategory of 'amiable' relations, distinguishing kinship from friendship with reference to the notion of consubstantiality (Pitt-Rivers, 1973). What Southwold means by congeniate relations is not entirely clear, but since congeniacy is defined with reference to familial relations, we may assume this concept to be close to that of Pitt-Rivers' notion of amiability, central to which is the notion of *altruism*. At the level of content, this provides us immediately with a contrast with economic relations which may be thought of as being essentially *egoistic*. However, the egoism of the economic applies only to exchange relations in a market economy. Hence the contrast is not with relationships universally involved in material production, but with the content of *market* relations. Relations of amity are therefore defined as the opposite of the relationships characteristic of the distinctively modern mode of production.

This opposition is an old one and belongs to the conservative reaction to the Enlightenment, which views modernity as subverting and destroying the world of interpersonal primary relations, and replacing them with secondary relationships characterized by egotistical calculation. The opposition between primary relations and secondary relations comes from Cooley. However, Cooley did not make the mistake of confusing primary relations with altruism and secondary relations with egoism. He insisted that primary groups, which he defined as groups which are 'fundamental in forming the social nature and ideals of the individual' (Cooley, 1963, p. 23), are no stranger to competition, self-assertion and the various appropriative passions. There is a danger that we interpret the term *affective* relationships as if it meant relationships characterized by *positive* effect. However, to claim that a relationship is affective, is simply to claim that the expression of *any* affect is not prohibited. The relationships of jealousy, hatred and rivalry are just as much affective relationships as those of amity. To specify altruism as a content of kin relationship flies in the face of all the ethnographic evidence to the effect that kin relationships are frequently characterized by hostility and competition. One is tempted to replace the term *amiable* relationships by *caring* relationships. However, while more correct, this is even more liable to misinterpretation than 'affectual'. The word 'care' suggests itself, however, because if one cares about another then what happens to them matters. To hate another is to care deeply about them – not in the sense of wanting what is best for them, but what is worst for them. Whatever the affect and mode of relationship, whether love and cooperation or hatred and competition, the fate of the parties to kin relationships is never a matter of indifference.

Rather than being distinguished by amiability, kin relations provide a diffuse social solidarity on the basis of which relations of amiability or hostility can arise, and Pitt-Rivers is certainly right to suppose that this solidarity is based on consubstantiality or what Giddings called 'consciousness of kind' (Giddings, 1922). However,

this is not only confined to kin relationships, but is also a characteristic of most ascriptive relationships from which kin relationships
differ in that they are personal and particularistic. It begins to seem
that if something of universal application can be said about the
content of kin relations, specification of content can only define
kinship relations in conjunction with some specification of their
form.

There is another argument against the attempt to specify the
content of kin relations in terms of altruism. Relationships subsist
between the occupants of social statuses conceived of as sets of
obligations or duties. To perform a duty is not necessarily to perform an act of altruism and the specification of duties serves to limit
the extent of an individual's obligation. The obligations of kinship
(in contrast to the formal and specific obligations created by content) are informal and diffuse. This fact can be adduced to show that
obligations between kin take the form of a generalized altruism
between the parties. However, the unspecified nature of kinship
obligations, in fact provides the opportunity for negotiation and
bargaining. Kin relationships, because they are mapped on to
genealogical relationships, form a network, and hence any one
person may typically claim a service from a number of kinsmen who
may negotiate among themselves as to who is to discharge the
obligation, such negotiations being very much concerned with individual advantage. However, if it is prohibited for kinsmen to put
their toes in the 'icy waters of egotistical calculation', this is because
of the inappropriateness not of self-interest but of calculation.

If kin relationships involve the conception of kin being in some
sense the same – all of a kind – then outside the familial/
reproductive domain kin relationships should be characterized by
equality between adults. Equality presupposes a social exchange: a
flow in one direction must be balanced by a flow in the reverse
direction. Hence the diffuse obligation of kinship may in practice be
modified by notions of exchange. Such notions, while not being
altruistic, fall far short of egotistical calculation. As many writers
have noted, kinship relations are not predicated on the desire of the
parties for individual benefit – they are not instrumental, but ends in
themselves. Consequently, the objective of exchanges between the
parties to a kin relationship does not involve the calculation of
advantage; it is rather concerned with the maintenance of an egalitarian social relationship.

However, this not to say that notions of advantage are inappropriate. The existence of a diffuse obligation based on social solidarity entails a high degree of trust, and the greater the degree of trust the longer may the period be between the two flows constituting an exchange. Hence though the notion of reciprocation does not involve equivalence as in an 'economic' transaction, nor is benefit from the exchange the basis of the relationship, notions of advantage are none the less involved. The recipient of a gift or favour from a kinsman is not required to reciprocate immediately, not because no reciprocation is involved but because the donor can *trust* the recipient to reciprocate if the occasion should arise. Conversely, by giving the gift the donor is building up a reserve of goodwill which he can have confidence he will be able to call upon.

Kinship relations involve exchange, but not equivalent exchange; they are concerned with advantage, but not the calculation of advantage. They constitute a field of relationships based on social solidarity and diffuse obligations which are structured by a history of past flows between members. In this respect, the benefit accruing to participants is analogous to that enjoyed by the members of an insurance scheme rather than to that enjoyed by the parties to a market exchange or the members of a joint stock company. Insurance schemes depend upon the fiduciary relation between members and an institution whose function is to create trust. Kinship *networks* are able to create the same effect without resort to the creation of institutional mechanisms, precisely because the network of relationships is drawn from a field of relationships characterized by social solidarity and diffuse obligation prior to any actual flows of benefits occurring.

Egoism and advantage are not foreign to kin relations. What is foreign is the *calculation* of advantage and *equivalent* exchange. It is therefore doubtful that they can be grouped with friendship relations under the more general notion of 'amity'. This is not, however, to deny that kin relationships are inherently moral, as Fortes has claimed, and as my own use of the term 'obligation' implies. Whether or not economic relationships in societies with capitalist modes of production are immoral is arguable. But they are certainly a-moral in the sense that no evaluation of actions or consequences take place in terms other than those of the morality intrinsic to market relations, i.e. the equivalence criterion. Morality and altruism are not identical. The latter involves giving preference by ego to alter's interests at the expense of his own. Whether that course of action is *right* (i.e. moral) depends on the judgement of whether in any given instance the realization of alter's interests constitutes a good.

However, progress towards specifying the content of kinship has to overcome yet another difficulty. That is, if we are referring (as we are) to kinship in the restricted sense (i.e. excluding descent), then kinship is universally bilateral. Each person is at the centre of a network of relationships which ramifies indefinitely and in which no two persons occupy the same position. This fact poses two problems. The first is that it is impossible, logically, to set any boundary to a person's kindred. In practice, any given ego's set of kin may be bounded by the past fact of intermarriage, and this is particularly likely to be the case in isolated settlements in the absence of out-migration. Any individual may by happenstance have a bounded set of kin. Such cases are likely to be rare and are entirely fortuitous. It is an essential part of the character of kinship that it is a device for the recognition of common kind, which precludes the possibility of demarcating a category of such kind. The second problem is that of genealogical distance or the 'fading' effect. A special class of obligations between kinsfolk are created by marriage and relations between the rearers and young reared together. Obligations constituting relationships which are not of this kind are weaker than those which are. If we concentrate on these weaker relationships, it soon becomes apparent that the strength of obligation tends to weaken or fade in proportion to genealogical distance. Williams (1956), in his study of a Cumberland village, notes that villagers refer to remote kin as 'some mak' o' forty second cousin'. Obligations to 'forty second cousins' tend to be less strong, more diffuse and less easily 'cashed' by the parties than, for example, obligations between a brother's son and a father's brother.

If we put these two problems together, then the kinship field of one individual is characterized by *a change in the character* of kinship relationships as one moves away from the individual at the centre towards the unmarked periphery. The closer the kin, the stronger are the obligations, the greater the difficulty of evasion, the smaller the possibility of negotiation, the greater the sanctions supporting fulfilment. Closer relationships have a *given* quality captured by the term 'ascribed'. Yet more distant relationships, while equally ascribed, are paradoxically frequently *chosen* on the basis of personal liking or consideration of advantage. A person may be motivated to perform a favour by the claim made by ego that he is a forty second cousin, while that degree of relationship is unclaimed and unrecognized in the cases of other forty second cousins whom ego dislikes for from whom he requires no favours. Such relationships may be those of friendship or patronage, be they economic or political or whatever, and are to be understood in those terms. *But*, the claim of kinship is crucial to their *establishment*. The description of them by participants as kin relationships is not merely an idiom. Methodologically, it is perfectly correct not to regard the mere establishment of genealogical relations between two related persons as the warrant for describing the relation as a kinship relation. It does not follow, however, that because the relation is comprehensible in substantive terms without reference to kinship, that it is not a kinship relationship and the reference to kinship merely an idiom imposed by the culture or the observer. The significance of kinship has to be established by examining the history of the relationship. The field of an individual's relationship needs to be seen not merely as a structure but as the product of a process in which the 'members' of the field are active in selecting 'partners' and deploying cultural resources and social knowledge to define the relationships which, at any given moment, constitute it.

This discussion of the character of kinship must be concluded with a more general consideration of the first problem arising from the bilateral nature of kin relationships. This a property of kinship which is frequently ignored in more general discussions of the topic. It is arguably more important than the biological reference, the cognitive function, the formal properties, the absence of universal substantive content (and hence of domain defining function), but it is none the less a property which clearly identifies kinship as 'pre-modern' – alien to those features which distinguish contemporary societies from their predecessors. Kinsfolk do not constitute a social group because they do not constitute a social category. There is no boundary which can be used to divide members from non-members. This characteristic is highly alarming to anyone used to conceptualizing the structure of a society in terms of the relationships between exclusive categories – classes, genders, ethnic and regional groups. The point here is not a cultural one, i.e. that kin relationships are particularistic and not universalistic, categorical ones; rather, it is a structural point. If kinship structures social relationships, it does not do so by virtue of category formation, let alone by the formation of categories whose members perform the same activity or function. It does so, rather, by generating social *networks*.

The essence of a social network is that it is composed of relationships of different kinds articulated in such a way that members are related not only directly but indirectly. It follows from this that actions performed in one relationship have implications for other relationships, so that the minimum unit of analysis is the triad rather than the dyad. It is to be hoped that it is unnecessary, given what has already been said in this chapter about the character of kinship, to warrant the claim that the network is the only possible structure which kin relationships could take given that character.

The fact that kinship generates a network is of the first importance for the way in which kinship functions and hence for its character. First, it provides members with choice as to what obligations they attempt to 'cash'. The claiming of kinship is not confined to distant kin. Even among close kin the actor is afforded a choice about which obligations to cash from whom. Secondly, it constrains actors. Claims made will affect the actor's relationships with relations other than the relation upon whom the claim is made. Moreover, both the claim and the response will be known to and sanctioned by other parties, since interconnectedness of the relationships constituting the network means that it has an important *communicative* function. The trust which is characteristic of kinship relationships is not due merely to their solidary nature, but also to the propensity of the network to ensure that commitments entered into by kinsfolk are discharged.

Only if the functional properties of networks are brought into the analysis can we avoid the naivity of supposing either that kin relationships are altruistic and devoid of the search for individual advantage or no different from the calculative egoistic instrumental relationships characteristic of societies dominated by secondary relationships. From the standpoint of the individual actor about to enter into a fiduciary relationship with another person related by kinship, it is no comfort to know that, *in general*, such relationships are characterized by diffuse solidarity and moral obligation. What he needs to know is whether the particular person in question will betray the trust, since kinship relations are no more exempt from the pursuit of individual advantage than any others. His security is assured not by an examination of the moral obligations involved in the relationship but by the effectiveness of the network in assuring that those obligations will be honoured.

For this reason, kinship relationships, rather than being inappropriate to economic life, in which fiduciary relationships play a major part, can constitute a major resource. The opposition between kinship and modern economic relationship at the formal level can lead us to misconceive the relationship between kinship and economic life, not only because they give a false character to kinship but also because they misconceive the character of economic life in contemporary society.

PART THREE

4

Family and Locality

The purpose of this part of the book is to discuss the significance of kinship in modern societies, focusing in particular upon Britain. The previous chapter, though restricted to kinship and ignoring descent, did not confine itself to a consideration of the character of kinship in modern societies. The emphasis on individual negotiation of relationships and their meaning did not derive from a particular concern with societies which are individualistic rather than collectivistic. That opposition is to be found within societies as well as between them – descent groups in pre-modern societies and families in modern societies being collectivities. Kinship, in contrast, is essentially individualistic, in that genealogical relationships individuate and do not classify. In every society, however collectivistic, the interests of individuals can always be distinguished from those of the group in theory and are separated in practice. Collectivistic societies are those which give primacy to the realization of collective interests over and against those of the individual. They are not societies in which individual interests and actions do not exist.

That having been said, we shall be concerned henceforth with kinship in societies with a high degree of the division of labour which is co-ordinated by markets and characterized by the values of individualism. Irrespective of whether they *need* be, such societies are in fact characterized by systems of nuclear family formation and the consequent distribution of households over a bewildering wide range of compositional types.

This is not the place to discuss the meaning of the term 'family': any remotely adequate treatment of this issue would require at least a chapter. It is sufficient for our purposes, however, to note that the term 'family' refers not to a category or an aggregate or network but to a social *group* which is formed by biological reproduction, and performs the functions of cultural reproduction or socialization and the daily reproduction of its members, in addition to the generational reproduction intrinsic to its central biological activity. It should not be referred to as *a* biological group, for it is just as much a cultural group; nor should it be referred to as '*the* biological group', a phrase which assumes that 'the family' is a natural phenomenon and therefore universal, an empirical issue which should not be prejudiced by definition.

The nurturance and rearing of children require the propinquity of rearers and reared. The reference to biological reproduction ensures that the rearers are the natural parents of the reared. Hence a family may be thought of as a group of persons residing in the same *place*, a group *composed* of parents and *immature* children. Given climatic conditions and all previous technology, daily reproduction requires shelter and facilities for food preparation. Hence family members will form not merely a residential group but a domestic group, and they will therefore share a common house and facilities, i.e. they will constitute a household. Not all residents of a dwelling necessarily form households, since mere residence in the same dwelling does not presuppose sharing of common facilities let alone a common housekeeping. Not all households, i.e. persons residing in the same dwelling and sharing housekeeping and facilities, are necessarily families, since not all such domestic groups are concerned with generational reproduction, but the members of any family (as it has been defined thus far) must constitute a household.

The family is therefore to be defined in terms of its activities; unlike kinship, where interaction and activity is predicated on the acceptance of claims to relationship, among family members relationship flows from activity. It follows that 'family' is not defined in terms of the set of relationships involved: the group is not defined in terms of its membership, or composition. Yet as we have seen, definition in terms of activity has *implications* for membership. However, any attempt to define 'family', whether in terms of relationships or activities, runs into difficulty, since the family is essentially a group defined with reference to a *process*. This process commences with the cohabitation of the mates and continues with the birth and raising of children, i.e. it involves changes in both activities and in the composition of the familial household.

The key problem that has to be solved in respect of the familial household is what happens when the children themselves take mates and engender children. In any given case it would be possible simply to add childrens' mates and their progeny to the original familial household. However, there cannot be either a societal rule or a general tendency for this to occur, since if it did then it would be a simple exchange of children, but no cohabitation between them. Hence we never find this pattern of residence. What we do find is a rule or a tendency for women *or* men to join their mates' households of origin. The household can in other words, *either* export daughters and import sons' wives or export sons and import daughters' husbands. When women are exchanged, the couple resides in the household of the male (termed *virilocal* residence), and where men are exchanged the couple resides in the households of the female (termed *uxorilocal* residence). There is, however, a third possibility, i.e. that upon mating, children of both sexes leave their households of origin and establish their own new household. This pattern is termed *neolocal* residence. These terms can also be applied to distinguish different types of residence when the young couple form a household of their own by shifting the terms' reference from household to district, from 'residence with' to 'residence near'.

What we have been discussing are the logical possibilities of forming new families; different principles of family *formation* which result in the formation of different types of *households*. Strictly speaking, the term 'nuclear family' refers to a *household* type as in the phrase 'nuclear family household'. In so far as it refers to a familial type, the type concerned is that of 'family formation', or 'family system'. To claim that modern societies are characterized by the predominance of the nuclear family is to claim that the normative pattern of family formation is *neolocal*. It is not to claim the predominance of a household type. Typically, newly married couples are not expected to start married life as part of the household of the parents of one of them, and typically an inability to establish an independent household is held to be a barrier to marriage.

If the formation principle is that on maturity of the children the household subdivides, it follows that a *nuclear family household* comprises parents and *immature* children. The nuclear family *household* is not to be confused with *the elementary family*. This term refers, not to a domestic group, but to a set of relationships which comprise the elements of the kinship system, i.e. all first degree (i.e. direct, unmediated) kin relationships. Of course, relationships found within nuclear family households are identical to those constituting the 'elementary family'.

We can therefore return to the definition of the family by distinguishing 'nuclear' and 'elementary' families and utilizing the notion of process. If we do so the term 'nuclear' is properly used to refer to a *stage* in the developmental cycle of the *elementary family*. We may say that a nuclear system of family formation is one in which the familial *household* subdivides or segments at the end of the nuclear stage of the elementary family's development.

The central issue then becomes: What happens to the elementary family in a nuclear system after it has passed through its nuclear stage? The first point to note is that the *relationships* constituting it do not dissolve. A woman, on marriage, is not freed from all obligation to her parents. Nor do the parties to the parent–child relationship suddenly lose all emotional significance for each other. The relationships endure beyond the point at which they cease to be domestic and residential relationships. It does not, however, follow that the members of the elementary family, once they cease to constitute a household, continue to constitute a group in the sense of acting together or having the capacity so to act, though they may do.

It follows that in a nuclear system, the nuclear household has a penumbra of extra-domestic *familial* relationships. The term 'familial' is used here in preference to the term 'family', since that term carries the connotation of there being relationships *within a family group*, which, we have seen, is not necessarily the case. 'Familial' is used in preference to 'kin' relationships to signal that much more is involved than diffuse solidarity based upon consciousness of kind. In addition, familial relationships are based upon intense interaction centred around events of primary ontological significance to the parties. It is therefore misleading to assimilate the relationships constituting this penumbra either to family relationships or to kin relationships in general.

In the literature on family and kinship in Britain, there is a tendency to describe these relationships as 'extended family' relationships. One reason for this usage is that these relationships vitally affect the internal working of the nuclear household and the behaviour of spouses has to be understood not only in terms of the membership of their nuclear household, but also in terms of their continuing relationships with the members of their elementary families of origin. I have argued elsewhere against this usage, as it leads to the supposition that, because spouses retain enduring relationships with their parents and siblings, the spouses' elementary families of origin, together with their common nuclear family, therefore comprise 'an extended family', i.e. a group composed of an elementary family and extensions of it by marriage and procreation. To avoid this error, I have proposed that the term 'extended kin relations' be preferred (Harris, 1983, p. 92). As will be evident from the above remarks, I now think this is a mistake: relations arising out of the experience of the membership of a family group have a different character from *other* kin relationships.

This distinction is important in understanding the significance of kinship in societies with nuclear systems of family formation. In such societies, evidence concerning the strength of extra-domestic *familial* relationships is often adduced as evidence concerning the continued importance of extra-domestic kin relationships in general.

Whether or not a post-nuclear elementary family continues to constitute a group and whether, in any given case, a nuclear family and the elementary families of origin of the spouses which overlap it constitute an extended family, the nuclear family household is never surrounded merely by a *set* of extra-domestic familial relationships: the relationships of each spouse at least necessarily constitute a network. Even if this network has a highly dense interaction pattern, it does not follow that its members can be said to constitute a group. The existence of such a network is not evidence of the existence of an extended family. However, the necessary existence of extra-domestic familial relationships and the fact that they constitute a network are, together, of great significance, not merely for the understanding of the functioning of family households, but also for the character of kinship in societies with nuclear family systems.

If the field of kin relationships constitutes a network, then the nodes of this network are 'families'. Indeed, the entire network may be seen as constituted by a series of overlapping elementary families; hence the frequent use of the expression 'family' as an alternative to 'kin'. It follows that the character of these relationships is affected by the character of family relationships. In other words, the necessity for distinguishing between familial and *other* kin relationships has to be balanced by the need to recognize the way in which *all* kin relationships have a 'familial' significance. These necessities can be rendered less paradoxical by distinguishing the form and content of relationships and between affective and cultural content. The disjunction between familial and other kin relationships concerns the manner of their establishment. Familial relationships arise out of reproductive activities involving interaction by persons living in proximity and are therefore emotionally charged. Other kin relationships have a primarily cultural significance which gives form to whatever content the relationship comes to have. This *cultural* significance or content is informed by the concepts and meanings which attach to the familial sphere. Hence both familial and other kin relationships have to be understood with reference to the meanings culturally associated with family relationships, but need to be distinguished in terms of their emotional content.

These considerations are relevant to the phenomenon of the 'fading' of kinship obligation with genealogical distance. The most stringent obligation exists between elementary family members, i.e. between members of past or present functioning groups. All other kin relationships involve weaker obligation, not because they subsist between members of different categories, but because the parties have never shared common household membership experiences. Two broad classes may be discerned within non-familial kin relationships: those between persons whose significance to each other is as members of known elementary families (or clusters thereof) and those between persons whose significance is primarily 'cognitive', i.e. occupying a place in a cognitive order.

Since this is, as far as I am aware, an original distinction, an ethnographic illustration is appropriate. In Wales, initial interaction between persons previously unknown to each other is typically concerned with what I shall term 'particularistic placing'. This involves establishing a connection between the parties by means of finding a member common to the social field of each. The simplest type of connection establishment involves ego locating alter as a member of an elementary family. For example, 'Oh, you're Joan Evans' mother', Joan Evans being a member of ego's social field, i.e. someone to whom ego is in some way connected. The most difficult and challenging form of connection establishment involves the establishment of a highly indirect link through people not necessarily known to either party. It may transpire that alter is ego's mother's mother's brother's wife's brother's son's son's wife's sister. This connection involves tracing the relationship through eight elementary families, of three of which the parties are likely to have no direct knowledge, and necessarily includes at least eight persons to whom no reference whatever will have been made in tracing the connection. Intermediate between these types are connections conceived of in terms of relations between families known to both parties. So it may be established that one of the Jones' (with whom ego has some connection) married an Evans and that their son married a Morgan with whom alter has a connection.

These three types of connection establishment parallel the three degrees of obligation. In the first case, what is significant is common elementary family membership between Joan and her mother; in the third, what is significant are the connections between known elementary families; in the second, the relations established serve to transform the relationship from that between stranger to that between placed persons, i.e. to fulfil a primarily cognitive function.

We have claimed that persons related by kinship 'matter' to each other. However, they can matter in different ways. Independently of the establishment of a personal relationship, persons remotely connected by kinship matter little. Persons related by familial kinship matter because of familial involvement rather than because of kinship recognition. The interesting category is the middle one. A sister's son matters because of the emotional involvement of the sister, and of the mother with the son, though the aunt lacks any direct emotional involvement with her nephew. The emotional significance of the nephew is the result of the juxtaposition of two familial relationships. Equally, grandchildren matter in the same way and the concern of grandparents to 'see' their grandchildren derives from a desire to transform this individual relationship into a direct one through interaction. Third-degree relationships, e.g. those between cousins (parents' sibs' children), are correspondingly less strong: they matter because the parent matters to ego, the sibs matter to the parent and the sib's child matters to the sib.

Now this explanation of the fading of kinship obligation with genealogical distance approximates to Malinowski's theory of the extension of sentiments. This theory failed to explain kinship in the large sense, i.e. it failed to explain the development of unilateral systems of descent, regarding them as the distortion of nature by culture. Here, however, we are not concerned with descent, but with the extension of sentiments in a bilateral system, to which the principal objections in Malinowski's theory do not apply. Moreover, we are not assuming that procreation universally results in the development of strong sentiments which are then extended; we are concerned only with the extension of sentiments in societies with nuclear systems of family formation. We are, however, making the assumption that strong sentiments are generated between elementary family members when reproduction is structured in a particular way, i.e. by the nuclear family formation, and that in such societies effective kinship derives from the extension of those sentiments.

Malinowski regarded sentiments as natural. It is no part of our purpose here to oppose the natural and cultural. To regard kinship relationships (as we have done) as being constituted by mutual obligation is to regard them as socioculturally constituted. The argument is, therefore, that the natural (i.e. spontaneous) sentiments generated by reproductive activities when they occur within nuclear family households, are culturally transformed into obligations and tied to family statuses. Similarly, those sentiments when extended to second- and third-order kin are likewise transformed and tied to kin statuses. Cultural prescriptions reinforce spontaneously generated sentiments and the general correspondence between prescription and sentiment makes the cultural prescription seem natural, thus leading us to see in exotic societies our own system of family and kinship on the grounds that being natural it must be universal. Hence, kin relationships have a familial meaning even when the emotional involvement characteristic of familial relationships is lacking. The whole field of kin relationships becomes diffused with familial significance; with the significance not of a cultural universal called 'the family', but with the meanings associated with 'family' in societies when reproduction occurs within nuclear family households.

Therefore, kinship, it may be argued, does have a specific cultural content in nuclear familial societies, but it remains, even so, without substantive content, since activities are not allocated on the basis of genealogical position and the obligations attached to such positions are diffuse and not specific. This is not to claim that because we cannot infer the content of kin relationships from our knowledge of the societal and family type, they do not as a matter of fact overlap with relationships belonging to substantive domains.

There is an analogy here with the contemporary family. While families are universally reproductive groups and units of consumption in British society, the principle of their formation is nuclear. As a matter of fact, families are frequently used to perform functions other than those of reproduction and consumption and to form groups wider than the elementary family. Whether an individual family *extends* its functions and composition in this way will depend on the social conditions under which it exists. When social conditions throughout a whole section of the society (region, class, occupational group) facilitate certain forms of extension, these are likely to become general and may permit us to speak of 'the' Lancashire family, 'the' working-class family, 'the' coal-mining family.

So it is with kinship. Kinship lacks any substantive content. It is not a domain. But, contingently, kin relationships do have a substantive content drawn from a social domain which they regularly structure in particular places and at particular times. Hence, to have no kin in the area in which you reside may have quite different consequences. It may indicate an absence of domestic services, or of access to information, or of political influence, or of custom, or of employment. The significance of kinship depends on which social domains kinship relationships structure, and that will vary from place to place.

The contribution made to our knowledge of kinship by community studies is frequently acknowledged by students of kinship in Britain. This is not an accident in the development of a discipline, but a consequence of a fact of great theoretical importance. 'Community studies' are better termed 'locality studies', since whether or not the object of study is a community and whether or not its character as a community is a focus of investigation, what the members of this *genus* of studies have in common is their concern with 'place'. They are concerned to abstract the systematic elements of social life which are peculiar to a particular *place*. They are concerned to show the contingent relations which have developed in that place between the elements of social structure. If kinship has no universal substantive content, even within societies of the same type, then its actual content will be the result of the development of contingent relations between it and particular social domains.

Methodologically, therefore, understanding kinship requires the comparison of the results of its study in particular places where it has a relationship to specific social domains, and it is material of this kind that community studies have provided.

But why should kinship be place-specific? Chapter 3 argued that, while not constituting a domain, kinship relations do have a distinct character; at the formal level they are diffuse, affective and personal relationships. This chapter has argued that they are also, in our type of society, diffused with a significance derived from the familial domain. However, purely cognitive relations cannot be substantively personal, nor is there likely to be much affect expressed between persons who merely know of one another rather than know one another as persons. The establishment of a field of persons known to be kin does no more than establish a field of potential personal relationships. In a society where people's kin fields are typically dispersed over a wide area, the interaction necessary to *establish* personal relationships will not take place.

It is important that this point should not be misunderstood. In the 1960s, it was strongly argued by certain American sociologists that distance was no bar to the maintenance of kin relations. However, the relations concerned were what we have termed extra-domestic familial relations, i.e. relationships which had already been established by co-residence. While distance need not be a barrier to the *maintenance* of a relationship, it remains, even in the late twentieth century, a barrier to its *establishment*, since establishment requires face-to-face interaction, and that in turn requires proximity, i.e. location in the same place.

In his study of kinship in London, Firth (1956) distinguishes between 'known' and 'recognized' kin. 'Knowledge' does not imply 'recognition'; it does not therefore imply the establishment of a personal relationship. Consequently, Firth (1956, p. 15) character-ized the British system of kinship as 'permissive' rather than prescriptive or obligatory. But what determines whether known kin relationships are activated? First-degree (elementary family) re-lationships are always activated because, in a nuclear family system, people related in that degree always co-reside at some point in their life course under conditions which involve interaction. But extra-familial kin do not necessarily ever reside in the same household or even locality. Hence, a necessary condition of the establishment of extra-familial kin relationships is propinquity. It is not a sufficient condition, however. Each individual can decide whether or not to claim or 'recognize' any relationship within his known and 'available' kin.

In small settlements where 'everybody knows everybody else', i.e. where the network of interaction is dense, available kin are likely to be known as persons quite irrespective of their kin relationship. In such cases, the existence of personal relationships between ego and a member of his available kin will be established independently of any claim to relationship. The knowledge of the relationship will constitute a resource available to the parties in their conduct of the relationship. Any piece of interaction or transaction is potentially capable of being interpreted as occurring between kinsfolk, and whether it is or not will result from the negotiation of its meaning by the parties.

In a 'permissive' system, structural factors determine *availability* of known kin but the constitution of the relationship as one of kinship results from the constructive activity of the parties. However, the content of the relationship will also depend on structural factors affecting the local population within which the relationship is found.

Spatial considerations are therefore central both to the recognition (i.e. establishment as opposed to maintenance) of kin relationships and to the determination of their content. It should not be imagined, however, that their importance is confined to rural settlements. Even in urban areas, the field of relationships is spatially structured, the degree of interconnection between the members of a person's social field being determined by their spatial articulation. Defined in terms of relationships, the social structure of any area may be thought of as a network whose nodal points are places: households, work establishments, associations. However, personal relationships arising from interaction in these settings only contingently outlast the cessation of that interaction. Because of their general character, namely the diffuse solidarity arising from the recognition of common kind, kinship relations can be maintained after interaction based on 'natural' (i.e. uncontrived) propinquity has ceased, thus extending the geographical range of ego's social field and hence the interconnectedness of the inhabitants of an area. Here the network character of the field of kin relationships is crucial. Kinship relations therefore perform a central function in articulating the social field of the population of an area.

How important this effect is, and how articulated is a given social field, will depend on the stability of the population over time; high rates of in-migration leading to low levels of articulation within the social field of the area and high rates of out-migration extending the range of social fields of individuals remaining within it.

So far, no mention has been made of the sort of meaning that recognition of common kind has in our culture, of the ideology of blood relations and the impact of the scientific knowledge of genetics on conceptions of kinship. This is a fascinating and neglected topic within family sociology, but it will not be discussed here because I do not believe it to be of central significance in understanding kinship relationships outside the familial sphere. If there is a sense in which extra-familial kin recognize each other and are recognized to be by others of common kind, and this sense is not that of common blood, what meaning does 'common kind' have in our type of society? To answer this question it is necessary, curiously enough, to refer once more to the spatial structuring of the fields of kin relations.

Kinship relationships are personal and particularistic and characterized by interaction on terms of equality. They also necessarily form a network. Networks have important communication functions. Kinship networks can of course communicate anything, but they are likely to communicate, in particular, personal information. To establish a relationship with a member of a network is, therefore, to gain accesss to the information that flows along it. Such information may be of considerable practical use. Whether it is of use or not, depends on whether the person to whom the information refers is a member or potential member of ego's social field. But a person's social field is spatially structured. Whether the information is of practical use will depend on the location of the person to whom it refers, and the usefulness of the network will depend on the degree of spatial overlap between it and ego's social field. In a permissive system kinship will be claimed if it can be used, and its usefulness will depend on the spatial structuring of the network of kin relations.

To understand the sense which 'common kind' has in modern society it is necessary to consider kinship in relation to its significance to non-kin. To be recognized by others as being a member of kin network is to be seen to partake of the character of the persons constituting it. The social reputation of a person depends 'on the company he keeps'; more precisely, it depends upon whom he or she interacts with on terms of equality. Kin relationships are egalitarian. Kin relationships are important in the constitution of a person's social identity. However, it must be remembered that the others engaged in the attribution of identity are necessarily not part of that person's kin network. Now, if that network is spatially dispersed it is unlikely that its members' character will be known to outsiders. Hence, a non-member will not be able to make an inference from the character of the kin of a person with whom he has contact, to the character of that person, since the character of the kin will itself be unknown. If, however, the network is spatially concentrated in a given area, it is likely that others will have independent knowledge of a person's kin and identify them as having the same social character. Ego will be identified by non-kin as being of the same social kind as his or her kin.

The particularistic placing characteristic of small settlements and of societies whose culture has been influenced by the life of such settlements, is therefore not merely a cognitive ritual; it has important practical significance. To establish a person's location is to establish the type of information to which he or she has access; it is also however, to establish their identity, their 'kind'. This kind has, however, two distinct elements. Ego's kin may be classified by others in terms of general categories, e.g. occupation, income, denomination, ethnic group. Particular relationships may be used to locate persons in universalistic categories. In such cases, ego may seek to remedy the defects in the knowledge of others in a manner calculated to provide some advantage – 'my brother, the head-master'; 'my cousin, the barrister'. Such strategies can however be self defeating since they may reflect adversely on the personal and moral qualities of ego.

This takes us to the second and insufficiently recognized function of placing, and that is the establishment of common kind in moral terms. People do not interact with categories but with members of categories. It is useful to know that ego's cousin is a plumber; but it then becomes necessary to ascertain whether the cousin is a good and reliable plumber, and judgements as to that are based on one's moral estimation of ego. Conversely, one's estimation of ego is affected by one's knowledge of his or her kin. This cannot occur if one does not know ego's kin personally, which is unlikely if they are spatially remote. This lack of knowledge cannot be remedied by ego. Ego's trustworthiness cannot be established on the basis of ego's own claim to have trustworthy kin.

At this point we encounter a difficulty. Establishment of social or moral identity through kinship is not like establishing identity through the identification of group membership, since ego's kinship network is logically unbounded, and within any given degree, not all kin (in a permissive system) will actually be recognized by ego. This consideration illuminates the problem of kin recognition. To claim kinship is not necessarily to claim rights *vis-à-vis* another. It is frequently to claim identity. Choice in the matters of kin recognition involves claims to identity as well as to obligation, but this choice is restricted by the degree of the other's knowledge of ego's genealogical kin. Those seeking a positive social identity may therefore be motivated either to remain near their kin or to migrate to escape negative identification. Kinship recognition is therefore neither given by genealogy nor freely chosen by ego nor even merely a matter of negotiation between genealogical kin. It is also a strategy employed in the negotiation of identity with non-kin. The degree of freedom in this negotiation diminishes as the degree of spatial concentration increases and the social consequences of such identification increase.

The degree of freedom involved in recognition might be thought to eliminate the utility of the use of kinship in establishing common kind. However, there are two memberships which a person cannot evade: that of his or her elementary families of origin and procreation. It should not be imagined that a person's 'kind' is therefore established by averaging the social or moral attributes of those kin relationships recognized by ego or known to others. Rather those relationships are traced by the establishment of links between elementary families, families which have their own collective reputations. Whether or not a post-nuclear elementary family remains a group, it certainly remains a category of evaluation. However, the elementary family can only function as a category of evaluation if there is, so to speak, a public among whom it is known, and this will depend once more on spatial considerations.

Kinship is not a field composed of a network of dyadic relations, but is structured by the interlocking of elementary family categories. It is not merely that the affective content of familial relationships is diffused throughout the system but also that the kind whose commonness is attributed to kinship derives from the nuclear family household itself and from its perceived function as manifesting or forming the social and moral character of its members. Just as the proximity of family members is central to the generation of strong affect, so is the spatial concentration of kin central to its function in the ascription of identity. At the same time the substantive content of extra familial kinship relations varies over space with the manner in which the different elements of social structure are locally articulated.

5

Kinship and Economic Life

Chapter 3 argued that if we restrict our attention to bilateral kinship and consider it as a *form* of social relationship, then it is possible to say something about its character or content despite the fact that such relationships do not define a domain of social activity. In formal terms, kinship relations may be seen as the opposite of modern market relations in societies with capitalist modes of production. Such relations are universalistic; in contrast, kinship relations are personal, diffuse, affective and based on particularistic ascription. They are characterized by a consciousness of common kind, whose members share a diffuse solidarity upon whose basis amiable or hostile personal relationships may arise. They are not necessarily characterized by altruism, nor are they foreign to the search for personal advantage and negotiation to secure it. They are, however, correctly termed moral relationships, since they are characterized by the existence of informal and diffuse obligations between the parties whose orientation is to the total person of the other, rather than to one social dimension or to performance. Their moral character does not mean that they are not characterized by exchange; rather, they contrast with economic relations in that they are not based on the norm of equivalent exchange but upon reciprocity over time made possible by the degree of trust engendered by their solidary nature. This degree of trust is enhanced by the structural properties of kinship relations which characteristically take the form of networks, the discharge of obligations being sanctioned by third parties. The network property, together with the unbounded nature of ego-centred kindreds, provides an individual with choice as to what obligations to honour and which kin to claim. Such decisions are explicable in part with reference to substantive considerations, i.e. the interests flowing from ego's activities. This does not imply that the relationship activated must be classified solely in substantive rather than kin terms. This depends on whether the relationship is established on the basis of claim to, and acceptance of, kin relatedness and obligation. Therefore, characteristically, kinship provides a basis for relationships, and constitutes a field within which exchange, negotiation and the search for personal advantage occur naturally.

Chapter 4 focused on the character of kinship peculiar to societies with nuclear systems of family formation and characterized by the separation of the institutional domains concerned with reproduction, with the maintenance of a symbolic order, with power and with the production, distribution and exchange of material goods. It argued the importance, in such societies, of distinguishing between relationships found within family groups (*family* relationships) and relationships subsisting between persons belonging to different groups but established through past memberships of the same group (*familial* relationships). It also argues the importance of distinguishing between *familial* relationships and *other extra-domestic kin relationships*, and distinguished within the latter category, relationships between persons whose significance depends on memberships of mutually known elementary families or clusters thereof and relationships which consist merely of a chain of dyadic relationships and perform a primarily cognitive function. It was then argued that in societies with nuclear systems of family formation, intense, affective relationships are generated between members of households concerned with reproduction, i.e. between persons who reside in the same place; that these relationships persist after the extinction of the nuclear household and that kin relationships of and beyond the second degree are diffused with the significance which attaches to relations between nuclear family household members in such societies. What is crucial here is the intense interaction based on proximity, rather than any natural sentiments universally generated by the reproductive process.

Because of their personal nature, propinquity was also seen to be a crucial determinant of the structure and function of extra-domestic kin relationships. The *establishment* (as opposed to maintenance) of substantively personal relationships between those formally personal relationships called 'kin', depends on propinquity, which is a major determinant of their availability. The activation of those relationships depends on their utility, which in turn depends on the activities of the potential parties to such relationships and the way those activities are structured. This differs between time and place, and therefore so does the content associated with kin relationships.

Propinquity determines availability because of the functions that kin relatedness performs. Kinship functions to establish the social identity and moral character of persons by virtue of their association with *known* others. Knowledge requires interaction and interaction is determined in large part by propinquity. Kinship will only be claimed for identity purposes if the kinsperson is known both to ego and to others constituting ego's 'public', and the fulfilment of this condition will depend on interaction and hence propinquity. Therefore, the number of claimed and activated relationships are likely to cluster spatially; hence the density of activated relationships, the operational density of interconnections between the members of a kin network, will be determined by the spatial clustering of its members. The greater the density, the greater control of members by the network, and hence the greater trustworthiness of its members. Central to the establishment of identity is elementary family membership, i.e. membership of a past or present group of a type which is culturally held to be, in Cooley's words, 'fundamental in forming the social nature and ideals of the individual'. But the character of such groups must be publicly known and this too will depend on propinquity.

If Chapter 3 has succeeded in diminishing the gulf assumed to exist between kinship and economic life, it may appear to the reader that Chapter 4 has widened it again. The whole point about a modern economy is that it is not local, nor even national, but international, and depends upon the space abolishing means of modern communication. Certainly 'the economy', the totality, is no longer domestic but global. However, so long as material goods are produced by the operation of people on material objects, there will of necessity be places of concentration of materials and concentrations of operatives around those locations to work them. If this is true of production, then similar considerations apply with even greater force to distribution; it is only in the sphere of exchange, in the sense of the transfer of the title to goods in exchange for money, that spatial considerations can be of little importance. As a result, productive and distributive enterprises are not distributed randomly in space but they are clustered, and around these clusters have grown up settlements, i.e. clusters of households which supply the enterprises with labour or labour services. Each enterprise draws on labour whose residence is within daily travelling distance of the enterprise, this being determined by the cost of travel and the opportunity cost of time spent travelling. As a result, the nodal points of networks, households and enterprises, tend to cluster together, and household, family and familial relationships become interarticulated and form a dense social field which forms the core of what may be termed a locality.

In economic terms, such localities constitute local labour markets, i.e. areas in which the inhabitants are potentially buyers or sellers of each other's labour power. The existence of such markets is the result of the *means* of production and distribution employed; but the relationships which define the area as a labour market are those of the capitalist *mode* of production, i.e. the capital–wage labour relationship. Such relationships are constituted by the labour *contract*. Labour contracts, as opposed to contracts concerned with material things, are very peculiar sorts of contract. What the employer wants is actual labour. What he gets in the labour contract is labour *power*, i.e. the title to actualize a generalized capacity to perform a type of labour. Once the contract is completed, therefore, he still has a problem, i.e. that of translating labour power into actual labour at those times and places where it is required. The labour contract initiates, therefore, an essentially political relationship between the employer and the employee and the structure of the work establishment is one of legitimate domination.

An employer is concerned initially with contracting a type of labour. He will be uninterested in applicants who do not belong to the relevant economic category. Conversely, workers will be concerned with the type of work and the levels of pay and conditions which are on offer. The labour contract creates, therefore, a classical 'modern economic' relationship based on contract not status, on membership of a general category, not on a particularistic relation; it creates a relationship whose membership is based on qualities which are achieved not ascribed, to which affect is irrelevant, whose significance is specific and which is entered into on the basis of the calculation of advantage. But it differs from 'pure' modern economic action in that it is not transitory like the making of a purchase, nor of short duration like a contract to deliver a given quantity of goods within a specified time period, but establishes a relationship which (if not terminated by an additional action of one of the parties) has an unlimited duration. The archetypal *relationship* established by a *contract* is not to be found in the economic domain at all. It is, of course, marriage.

Now, the analogy with marriage should not be pursued too far. However, in both cases, the parties are concerned as to how the other will perform after the contract has been established, even though they may have prudently assured that the other party belongs to all the right general categories. Performance depends on who they are; it can be inferred both from their social identity and moral reputation, i.e. it depends upon attributes which differentiate persons within the same general category. The employer will require of employees that they be honest, sober, diligent, punctual, cooperative and willing to actualize their inherent capacities on demand. The worker will require that employers also be honest, fair and reasonable in the interpretation of employees' duties. The employer has, however, a disadvantage when compared with workers in the assessment of personal qualities. Employers are few and have relatively easily ascertainable public reputations. Workers are many and lack public reputations. Employers, unlike suitors, do not have time to enjoy lengthy courtships before tying the knot. They therefore need a short-cut to establish the social identity of job applicants. This is provided by ascertaining ascriptive category membership, the reputation of the ascriptive category substituting for personal reputation and leading to discrimination in recruitment against culturally unfavoured categories which may on occasion be those of Catholic/Protestant, Jew/Gentile, black/white, male/female, young/old. But this strategy merely substitutes one general category for another. An alternative or additional strategy is to make an inference from the known to the unknown, and to use employees whose capacities and character are known to recruit others of the same kind. The prudent employer will, of course, want to be certain that an employee who recommends a worker for employment does indeed possess the personal knowledge required, and such a claim is doubly warranted in the case of kin: kin will be both personally known and morally bound to the employee as well as presumptively of the 'same kind'.

The importance of kinship as a subsidiary principle of labour recruitment derives, not from a concern with their ascribed and particularistic qualities, but from a concern with performance which the Parsonian scheme rightly emphasizes. The weakness of that scheme, upon which the error in Parson's argument is consequent, is that it assumes that performance is uniquely predicted by category membership, when in fact it is additionally determined by the personal qualities of category members which cannot be established (without lengthy interviewing procedures) by formal methods of recruitment.

The resort by employers to the use of kinship as a subsidiary principle of labour recruitment is well documented, though less in the kinship literature than in the literature on labour markets, redundancy and job search. This literature has recently been reviewed by Grieco (1987). However, it has often been ignored by students of kinship. Grieco's distinctive contribution is however, to document the way in which kinship can be used as a principle of labour recruitment over distance and the central importance of kin aid in facilitating migration. The implication of this work is that kinship need not be important in labour recruitment merely in areas of residential stability.

Employer recruitment procedures have a consequent effect on the behaviour of workers in the market outside the work establishment and on the importance of kin ties. Rather than making a formal application for work, they will seek information about job opportunities through kin and then seek to make their applications successful by persuading kin already employed to 'speak for' them to the employer. When kin relationships perform this function they acquire an instrumental and economic significance. Though kin relationships can aid migration to employment, they are more likely to have this significance in local labour markets with relatively stable populations, where market conditions provide the employer with a degree of choice and among low-status occupational categories. The association with low-status categories derives from two considerations. First, the ratio of the costs of sophisticated recruitment methods to the value of the labour recruited will be high in such categories. Secondly, among lowly skilled workers, performance will be more strongly determined by personal qualities than category membership. To put this point a different way, kinship is most likely to have a labour market function among the 'traditional working class'.

There is a danger that this fact be used to warrant the claim that 'labour market' kinship is an archaic (and disappearing) phenomenon associated with yesterday's industrial societies and alien to the post-modern societies of today. The matter is not, however, that clear-cut. All sectors of industrial society never conformed to the paradigm of modernity; nor do all sectors of contemporary society conform to a paradigm of post-modernity. The succession of historical characteristics do not displace one another, but are rather added to one another. In any case, since post-modern economies are characterized by labour displacement, industrial restructuring and rapid rates of firm formation and dissolution, among the working class the experience of the actual selling of labour power is likely to figure more prominently than in the past. Despite tight labour market conditions in some regions of the Western world, it would be audacious in the extreme to claim that the future is one of full employment in which employers can exercise little choice.

While trust is involved in the recruitment of labour – the employer trusts the employee who recommends a kinsperson whom they trust – the employer–employee relationship is not a fiduciary one. Management – worker relations within the work establishment are relations of domination, monitoring and control, not trust. However, relations between the Board and management, while formally those of employer and employee, have a fiduciary element because of the necessary autonomy and discretion accorded to managers. It is not surprising to discover, therefore, that kinship is frequently used in both the recruitment of Board members and management. Exchange relations are essentially fiduciary, since the time-lapse between contract and fulfilment of its terms allows for default.

Whenever relations of trust are involved in economic life, considerations arise which are similar to those involved in employee recruitment. While categorical considerations are of prime significance in estimating performance, personal characteristics are also central. Where personal characteristics are central, so are ascriptive category membership, social identity, moral reputation and network control. Where structural conditions are appropriate, kinship is likely to be employed therefore in the selection of partners in both production and exchange.

It may be argued, therefore, that personal relationships necessarily play an important part in economic life. This has the

implication that there is something very wrong with characterizations of 'the economic' which represent it as the opposite of
personal relations in general and kin relations in particular, and
with characterizations of kinship which define it as the opposite of
the economic. This error is in part the result of confusing the
separation of distinct institutions – political, economic, etc. – with
the separation of their corresponding social aspects, identifying the
personal with the reproductive institutional domain, and assuming
that any social relationship must belong unequivocably to one social
sphere. It is also, in part, the result of failing to distinguish between
typical and actual relationships and between the establishment and
conduct of a relationship. Typical *economic* relationships are not
established on the basis of personal ties between the parties. Typical
personal relationships are not established on the basis of economic
category membership. But *specific* economic relationships may be
established on the basis of personal ties, and *specific* personal
relations may be *used* for economic purposes.

There is a sense, however, in which these criticisms do not get to
the heart of the matter. The conventional characterization of
economic life presupposes that economic relations are governed by
a set of norms to which the norms governing kinship relations are
inimical. In so doing, it fails to distinguish cognitive from normative
considerations. If when wishing to employ a plumber one is
concerned to categorize applicants in terms of their knowledge and
experience of plumbing, this not because one believes that is how
one ought to behave in an economic relationship, but because such
categorization is a pragmatic necessity if one wants plumbing to be
done. The imperative is hypothetical not categorical. It follows that
there is nothing shocking, wicked or disgusting in preferring a
suitably qualified kinsperson whom one can trust and control to a
suitable, qualified stranger, especially if this self-regarding action
can be represented as a discharge of a moral obligation to the
kinsperson concerned and used to elicit equally advantageous
reciprocation on a future occasion. To appoint an unqualified
kinsman on the grounds of kinship obligation would be regarded by
all the parties concerned not as wrong but as stupid. Normative
considerations are involved here, of course, but the norm is that of
rationality, which emphasizes the cognitive mode as opposed to the
appreciative or moral. To appoint a man as a plumber who had not
the requisite skills would indeed be shocking; but it would also be

shocking to appoint a man whom one could not trust in preference to one whom one could.

Practical activities engender relationships which have a predominantly cognitive orientation. But kinship relationships are not engendered by a class of activities and hence the orientations of the parties to such relationships must be appreciative or moral. But the moral character of kinship has consequences for the performance of practical activities since their successful accomplishment depends on the faithful cooperation of persons. Social relationships are concrete relations between both categories *and* persons and the qualities of each conditions the other. Hence, not only can kinship ties operate to establish or sustain economic relationships, but economic relationships can strengthen or weaken kinship ties; kin ties crossing economic category boundaries being weakened by economic differentiation and ties within categories being strengthened by the addition of the diffuse solidarity engendered by common class or occupational category membership to that associated with kinship.

Economic relationships are misconceived as being in practice unidimensional relationships between category members. It is tempting at this juncture to claim that such relationships are psychologically intolerable and hence are always humanized; that actual relationships in the economic domain involve an uneasy balance between rival tendencies to depersonalization and personalization. This humanistic temptation must be stoutly resisted, because the assumption that the dynamics of economic life in market societies involves a tendency to depersonalization, leaves unchallenged the opposition between economy and kinship when conceived of as an opposition between the categorical and the personal. The point is, rather, that economic activity itself produces tendencies towards personalization.

The depersonalization 'thesis' is on strongest ground when it focuses not on relations between members of productive groups, but upon *market* relations, which are inherently competitive, calculative and advantage-seeking. Durkheim was the first to point out that such relationships have an irreducible moral component without which they could not function. The claim being made here is that they have an irreducible 'personal' component without which they could not function.

The ideology of the free market proposes that the good of the greatest number is achieved under conditions of maximum competition, and that these conditions are achieved by the removal of institutional and other non-economic constraints on the freedom of individuals to seek maximum advantage. The conclusion is then drawn that if constraints are removed, individuals will be motivated in such a way as to move the market in the direction of 'maximum' or 'perfect' competition. However, the unmitigated pursuit of individual interest does and will not result in movement towards perfect competition. It is in the interest of sellers, whether of labour or of other commodities, to restrict the degree of competition by exercising some form of social closure which will enable them to exclude new entrants and control prices themselves and not let their determination result from market mechanisms. It is that same self-interest which is postulated as the driving force of market-oriented economic action, not archaic survivals from pre-market social forms, altruistic moralities or humanistic values, which is responsible for 'imperfections' of markets. Weber (1978, p. 638), makes a cognate point in the following terms:

> Capitalistic interests thus favour the continuous expression of the free market but only up to the point at which some of them succeed . . . in obtaining for themselves a monopoly for the sale of their products or the acquisition of their means of production, and in thus closing the market on their own part.

Following Weber, Murphy (1988) has argued against Collins (1975) that 'most of the departures from the pure model of open market competition result from market competition itself' (Murphy, 1988, p. 69).

Social closure theory as advanced by Parkin (1974), Collins and Murphy is a theory of stratification which is still contested. What is uncontested, and often neglected, is the importance of social closure in social life. Social processes do not merely unite, create solidarity and include; they divide, create opposition and exclude. If societies are conceived of as structures generated by the relations subsisting between social categories, this must be so. A category with no non-member has little practical value. Hence categories necessarily serve to exclude as well as include. Social differentiation does not merely result from the development of the division of labour, but it is the precondition of any form of social order.

Since social closure theory is a theory of stratification, it is concerned with the exercise of social closure by social categories. From the standpoint of such a theory, economic phenomena may be seen as being modified by the operation and non-economic criteria, e.g. in the actions of status groups. These rather simplistic interpretations of Weber do, of course, leave the 'modern economic'–non-economic dichotomy untouched. The point being made here is that the motivation to use 'non-economic' criteria in economic action derives from the economic system itself, and extends beyond categorical relationships to personal ones.

The continued significance of kinship in contemporary society is frequently understood in terms of what kin can do for each other. Hence, it has been well-established that kin provide domestic services, information about housing and job opportunities, act as sources of influence, and so on. This tradition can be criticized for focusing too narrowly on kin to the exclusion of kinship. However, even on its own terms, it is inadequate if it ignores non-kin. The channelling of information to some persons *and not others*, means that others are excluded from the receipt of that aid and information. Because of the properties of bilateral kinship, kin will not constitute a bounded group; because of the networked character of social relations, aid and information will be available through other types of links in the network. However, because of their informational and fiduciary character, kin links in the network will be used in preference to other equally available types of link, and this will serve to restrict resource flows to the benefit of kin.

It is not being claimed that in the economic life of contemporary societies kin operate mechanisms of social closure: closure can only by exercised by bounded categories or groups. What is being claimed is that not only in the sphere of production, but also in that of exchange, the pursuit of individual advantage leads individuals to attempt to restrict resource flows in order to modify the degree of competition, and that, in general, ascriptive qualities – and in particular kin relatedness – provide the criteria for such restriction. Restriction is the first stage in the establishment of monopoly, i.e. full social closure, which may be regarded therefore as a special case of the more general phenomena of restriction. Economic life in market societies may be regarded as being characterized by attempts at restriction, which in some cases may result in monopoly and closure, and kinship is a resource for such restriction.

The use of kinship as a criterion of restriction should not be confused with the use of kinship as a principle of group formation. In market societies with bilateral systems of kinship, the struggle for closure cannot be understood as taking place between kin groups, i.e. between groups defined in kin terms. One is tempted to make this error because of a quite different function of kinship, and that is the intergenerational transmission of monopoly or privilege, whether the monopoly be of property or office. The distinction between restriction and transmission is of course cognate with the distinction between extrafamilial and familial kin. The family is a reproductive group and one of the things that it reproduces is monopoly or privilege. Members of groups defined in these terms will seek to use ties of filiation to transfer resources to the next generation. That generation will then share an identity with the previous generation on two counts; they will share both a common position in the economic order, a categorical identity, and that identity resulting from their particularistic relation to the previous generation, a personal identity. They will be doubly of common kind. However, they will not be economically privileged because they belong to a kin group, but because of their ties of filiation to members of an economic group.

However, intergenerational preservation of privilege requires that the flow of resources between generations is restricted in such a way so that not only is closure pursued, but also that *concentration* is maintained. Hence property must not be dispersed by intermarriage with the propertyless. As a result, marriage with other members of the economic category will be preferred, thus leading to the establishment of kin ties between the elementary families that compose it. The members of the economic category will, therefore, by the third generation, become members of a kin network which is bounded, being closed at the boundary of the economic category. From then on, closure can be represented in kin and identity rather than economic terms, and what is essentially an economic group can be described as a kin group. Once this has occurred, kin relations will be used to restrict competition between members of the group and as a resource in that competition itself. This is possible because the permissive nature of the kinship system and the 'fading' of kinship obligations with genealogical distance, allows scope for the negotiation of recognition according to the material interests of the potential parties.

Many descent groups in simple societies are exogamous. Where relations between descent groups are hostile, their members say 'we marry our enemies'. This has the consequence that the division between opposing descent groups is balanced by their connection by bilateral ties of kinship. In market societies, even the members of privileged groups are competitors. The members of such groups may say 'we marry our competitors'. The kinship interconnection of the members of privileged groups in market societies then acts as a principle of solidarity, secondary to that of 'class' interest which modifies countervailing tendencies to disintegration resulting from the internal competition among class members.

This example from the area of stratification exemplifies the paradoxical character of kinship and the relationship between kinship and economic life. Kinship is not a domain: it stands in opposition both to the 'family', the substantive domain of generational reproduction, and to the 'economy', the substantive domain of the production and exchange of material goods. However, the need to reproduce the material advantage through the mechanism of the family leads eventually to the kin connectedness of the members of an economic category, providing it with a social identity and forming solidarity which reinforces that deriving from the sharing of a common type of material interest.

Kinship has no substantive content and, being bilateral, cannot be used to form exclusive social categories. Hence, common kind is specified by a substantive content deriving from the domain which it overlaps. The criterion of category membership lies in the field of content, and does not derive from the form of kin relationships themselves. The establishment of the category derives from the existence of substantive economic, and not formal kinship criteria. The maintenance of the category over generations and its transformation into a solidary group depends on the establishment of a network of interpersonal kinship relations between members which becomes closed at the category boundary, thus permitting its social redefinition as a kin, rather than an economic, group.

Kinship relationships are moral, expressive and given, not calculated, instrumental and chosen. This does not mean that they only subsist between persons who share common interests and are characterized by altruistic actions. On the contrary, they are the means of the pursuit of individual advantage, they are employed as a resource in competitive struggles, and they are claimed and recognized on the basis of mutual individual interest. They serve not only to transmit but to restrict the flow of resources, thus sharpening the competitive advantage of kin at the group boundary, but diminishing the rigours of interpersonal competition within the group itself.

Both Parsons and Marx were correct to identify the character of modernity as being constituted by the centrality of categorical relationships for social structure, and Parsons was correct to conceive of kinship (which preceded categorical, 'class' relationships as a principle of social structure) as the logical opposite of class relations. Both social theorists and students of kinship, by identifying kinship too closely with the familial, have tended to assume that the functional separation of productive and reproductive institutions implies the segregation of kin relationships from the economic sphere and have identified kinship too closely with affectivity and ignored its cognitive properties. In addition, Parsons has wrongly identified the universalistic imperative as categorical rather than hypothetical. The net result has been the mistaken empirical inference that kinship plays no part in economic life, for which it is held to be *dys*functional and to which it is seen to be opposed at the normative level.

This error parallels the vulgar error of supposing that economic life and religion constitute different spheres, an error which Weber's work substantially disposed of by showing the consequences of religious belief for economic action. However, it has not been a part of the argument of this book that kinship ideology has consequences for economic action. Rather, this book has argued that kin relationships structure economic relations, not only because social relationships are both categorical and personal, but also because kin identification buttresses categorical placement as a means to the prediction of economic performance. Kinship is, therefore, and will continue to be, a potential and frequently utilized element in the structure of economic relations, and therefore of lasting significance even in market societies with nuclear systems of family formation.

References

Barnard, A. and Good, A. (1984). *Research Practices in the Study of Kinship*. London: Academic Press.

Barnes, J. A. (1961). Physical and social kinship. *Philosophy of Science*, **28**, 296–9.

Beattie, J. H. M. (1964). Kinship and social anthropology. *Man*, **64**, 101–3.

Bloch, M. (1973). The long term and the short term: The economic and political significance of the morality of kinship. In J. Goody (Ed.), *The Character of Kinship*, pp. 75–88. Cambridge: Cambridge University Press.

Collins, R. (1975). *Conflict Sociology*. London: Academic Press.

Cooley, C. H. (1963). *Social Organisation*. New York: Shocken Books.

Dumont, L. (1971). *Introduction à deux theories d'anthropologie sociale*. Paris: Mouton.

Feleppa, R. (1986). Emics, etics, and social objectivity. *Current Anthropology*, **27** (3), 243–51.

Firth, R. (1956). *Two Studies of Kinship*. London: Athlone Press.

Fortes, M. (1953). The structure of unilineal descent groups. *American Anthropologist*, **55**, 17–41.

Fortes, M. (1969). *Kinship and the Social Order*. Chicago: Aldine. Page numbers refer to the 1970 edition. London: Routledge and Kegan Paul.

Gellner, E. (1957). Ideal language and kinship structure. *Philosophy of Science*, **24**, 235–42.

Gellner, E. (1960). The concept of kinship. *Philosophy of Science*, **27**, 187–204, Reprinted in Gellner, E., *The Concept of Kinship*, pp. 163–82. Oxford: Blackwell, 1973.

Gellner, E. (1963). Nature and society. *Philosophy of Science*, **30**, 236–51. Reprinted in Gellner, E., *The Concept of Kinship*, pp. 183–203. Oxford: Blackwell, 1973.

Gellner, E. (1973). *The Concept of Kinship*. Oxford: Blackwell.

Giddings, F. H. (1922). *Studies in the Theory of Human Society*. New York: Macmillan.

Goody, J. (Ed.) (1973). *The Character of Kinship*. Cambridge: Cambridge University Press.

Grieco, M. (1987). *Keeping it in the Family*. London: Tavistock.

Harris, C. C. (1983). *The Family and Industrial Society*. London: Allen and Unwin.

Kroeber, A. L. (1909). Classificatory systems of relationship. *Journal of the Royal Anthropological Institute*, **39**, 77–84.

Kuper, A. (Ed.) (1977). *The Social Anthropology of Radcliffe-Brown*. London: Routledge and Kegan Paul.

Kuper, A. (1983). *Anthropology and Anthropologists*. London: Routledge and Kegan Paul.

Kuper, A. (1986). The man in the study and the man in the field. *European Journal of Sociology*, **21** (1), 14–39.

Lévi-Strauss, C. (1969). *Elementary Structures of Kinship*. London: Eyre and Spottiswoode.

Malinowski, B. (1930). Kinship. *Man* **30** (17).

Malinowski, B. (1935). *Coral Gardens and their Magic*. London: Allen and Unwin.

Marshall, T. H. (1934). Social class: A preliminary analysis. *Sociological Review*, **26** (1). Reprinted in Marshall, T. H., *Citizenship and Social Class*. Cambridge: Cambridge University Press, 1950.

McLennan, J. F. (1876). *Studies in Ancient History*. London: Bernard Quaritch.

Morgan, L. H. (1870). *Systems of Consanguinity and Affinity*. Washington, D.C.: Smithsonian Institution.

Morgan, L. H. (1877). *Ancient Society*. New York: Henry Holt.

Murphy, R. (1988). *Social Closure*. Oxford: Clarendon Press.

Needham, R. (1960). Descent systems and ideal language. *Philosophy of Science*, **27**, 96–101.

Needham, R. (1971). Remarks on the analysis of kinship and marriage. In R. Needham (Ed.), *Rethinking Kinship and Marriage*, pp. 1–34. London: Tavistock.

Needham, R. (Ed.) (1971b). *Rethinking Kinship and Marriage*. London: Tavistock.

Parkin, F. (1974). Strategies of social closure in class formation. In F. Parkin (Ed.), *The Social Analysis of Class Structure*, pp. 1–18. London: Tavistock.

Parsons, T. (1949). *The Structure of Social Action*. Glencoe: Free Press.

Parsons, T. (1951) *Towards a General Theory of Action*. Glencoe: Free Press.

Pitt-Rivers, J. (1973). The kith and the kin. In J. Goody (Ed.), *The Character of Kinship*, pp. 89–106. Cambridge: Cambridge University Press.

Radcliffe-Brown, A. R. (1935). Patrilineal and matrimonial succession. *Iowa Law Review*, **20**, 286–303. Reprinted in Radcliffe-Brown, A. R., *Structure and Function in Primitive Society*, pp. 32–48. London: Cohen and West, 1952.

Radcliffe-Brown, A. R. (1941). The study of kinship systems. *Journal of the Royal Anthropological Institute*, **71**. Reprinted in Radcliffe-Brown, A. R., *Structure and Function in Primitive Society*, pp. 49–89. London: Cohen and West, 1952.

Radcliffe-Brown, A. R. (1951). Systems of kinship and marriage. In A. R. Radcliffe-Brown and D. Forde (Eds), *African Systems of Kinship and Marriage*. Oxford: Oxford University Press. Reprinted in A. Kuper (Ed.), *The Social Anthropology of Radcliffe-Brown*, pp. 189–286. London: Routledge and Kegan Paul, 1977.

Radcliffe-Brown, A. R. (1952). *Structure and Function in Primitive Society*. London: Cohen and West.

Rivers, W. H. R. (1914a). *Kinship and Social Organisation*. London: Constable.

Rivers, W. H. R. (1914b). *History of Melanesian Society*. Cambridge: Cambridge University Press.

Schneider, D. M. (1965). The nature of kinship. *Man*, **64** 180–81.

Schneider, D. M. (1968). *American Kinship: A Cultural Account*. Englewood Cliffs, N.J.: Prentice-Hall.

Schneider, D.M. (1972). What is kinship all about? in P. Reining (Ed.), *Kinship Studies in the Morgan Centennial Year*, pp. 32–63. Washington, D.C.: Anthropological Society of Washington.

Schneider, D. M. (1984). *A Critique of the Study of Kinship*. Michigan: University of Michigan Press.

Southwold, M. (1971). Meanings of kinship. In R. Needham (Ed.), *Rethinking Kinship and Marriage*, pp. 35–56. London: Tavistock, 1971.

Weber, M. (1978). *Economy and Society* (edited by G. Roth and C. Wittich). Berkeley: University of California Press.

Williams, W. M. (1956). *Gosforth*. London: Routledge.

Name Index